PENGUIN BOOKS

DAD RULES

Andrew Clover used to read books about Russian people who discover, after a long, long, long time, that life is bad. He now reads books about sheep who like hiding behind bushes. These books are much better. You can lift the flap and find a sheep. With the other books, you can't lift a flap and find a Russian. He does the 'Dad Rules' column at the back of the *Sunday Times Style* magazine. He is a comedian, writer and trophy husband. He lives with his wife, his three daughters and a female dog. Yes, that's a lot of women. In his house, he never rules.

D1386944

Dad Rules

*How My Children Taught
Me to be a Good Parent*

ANDREW CLOVER

PENGUIN BOOKS

PENGUIN BOOKS

Published by the Penguin Group
Penguin Books Ltd, 80 Strand, London WC2R 0RL, England
Penguin Group (USA) Inc., 375 Hudson Street, New York, New York 10014, USA
Penguin Group (Canada), 90 Eglinton Avenue East, Suite 700, Toronto, Ontario, Canada M4P 2Y3
(a division of Pearson Penguin Canada Inc.)
Penguin Ireland, 25 St Stephen's Green, Dublin 2, Ireland (a division of Penguin Books Ltd)
Penguin Group (Australia), 250 Camberwell Road,
Camberwell, Victoria 3124, Australia (a division of Pearson Australia Group Pty Ltd)
Penguin Books India Pvt Ltd, 11 Community Centre,
Panchsheel Park, New Delhi – 110 017, India
Penguin Group (NZ), 67 Apollo Drive, Rosedale, North Shore 0632, New Zealand
(a division of Pearson New Zealand Ltd)
Penguin Books (South Africa) (Pty) Ltd, 24 Sturdee Avenue,
Rosebank, Johannesburg 2196, South Africa

Penguin Books Ltd, Registered Offices: 80 Strand, London WC2R 0RL, England

www.penguin.com

First published by Fig Tree 2008
Published in Penguin Books 2009
1

Copyright © Andrew Clover, 2008
Illustrations copyright © Andrew Clover, 2008
All rights reserved

Extract on page 279 from *The House at Pooh Corner*, text by
A. A. Milne, © The Trustees of the Pooh Properties. Published by
Egmont UK Ltd London and used with permission

The moral right of the author has been asserted

Typeset by Rowland Phototypesetting Ltd, Bury St Edmunds, Suffolk
Printed in England by Clays Ltd, St Ives plc

Except in the United States of America, this book is sold subject
to the condition that it shall not, by way of trade or otherwise, be lent,
re-sold, hired out, or otherwise circulated without the publisher's
prior consent in any form of binding or cover other than that in
which it is published and without a similar condition including this
condition being imposed on the subsequent purchaser

ISBN: 978-0-141-03371-6

www.greenpenguin.co.uk

Mixed Sources
Product group from well-managed
forests and other controlled sources
www.fsc.org Cert no. SA-COC-1592
© 1996 Forest Stewardship Council

Penguin Books is committed to a sustainable future
for our business, our readers and our planet.
The book in your hands is made from paper
certified by the Forest Stewardship Council.

Why I've Written This Book

It's a Saturday. I'm standing in Foyles bookshop, and I find three walls of parenting manuals. There's one – two hundred pages long! – called *Everything You Need To Know* (*in the first months of a child's life*). I'm thinking: Is there that much I should have known? I have, twice, lived through a child's first months. I could boil my experience down to three sentences of advice:

1. Don't be reading two-hundred-page books. Try to sleep.
2. Don't let them suck too long, or mum's nips will really hurt.
3. Get out the way when they puke.

I find several glossy volumes, which originated on TV, so they do what TV does best: concentrate on the freaks. I open the first book. It plunges me into a world of chaos and fear. I'm smelling the sick stuck to the seatbelt. The next one features photos of Supernanny, who's clearly been styled by a whole team of Style Experts, so she looks strict but sexy – like a frisky Mary Poppins, who'd wipe your surfaces, then give you a spanking. I want to push Supernanny in a big muddy puddle. The childcare guides are making me feel depressed, and angry, and inadequate. I leave.

I head homewards, and find Liv in the park with the girls. She goes straight off to make lunch. People say kids bring parents together. They do, for about sixty seconds – the length of the average handover. At the playground, all the parents seem to have been reading the same books I have. The mums are mainly looking furious. Their body language is screaming: 'If ANYONE else asks me to do something, I will start screaming, and I won't stop.' The dads are worse. They are trying to make phone calls, and are getting tetchy because they're losing the connection. Or they're following their kids saying 'Careful, Molly!' with that silly, soppy expression on their faces, like they want to play, but they are embarrassed.

I feel really depressed. I'm thinking: What's the point of life? What's the point of kids? They shout at night, they drain all your money and then they leave and blame you for everything that goes wrong with their lives.

At this point Cassady arrives. My second daughter. She's three and a half. She's wearing blue pants on her head. She's pulling the rope of this brilliant go-kart we've got. My humming granddad made it fifty years ago out of wooden orange crates and two pram wheels. Cassady says: 'Daddy, we *need* to get to our castle. You are a magic horse and you are called Barry the Magic Horse and you've got BIG BLACK HAIRY HOOVES!' My daughter is very forceful. It's like dealing with Paul McKenna, disguised as a small girl.

I immediately start to feel quite horsey. The other daughter arrives. Grace. The lanky one. She's five. She steps gingerly into the go-kart. They both shout, 'Giddy-up, Daddy! Giddy-up!'

I grab that go-kart, and I canter off at some speed. As I leave the playground, I do a neiiiigggggghhh of pleasure. They cheer. I gallop off down the woodland path. I'm seized by a moment of horsey pleasure. I leap over a tree trunk, for the sheer joy of it.

Then I realize I'm out of breath. I walk. I think: How did

those little witches get me to pull them home? I turn and look at them. They're doing clip-clop noises and singing that mad song they learned at school, the one where they chant: 'Brush your teeth with bubblegum! Belly flop in a pizza!' They are happy. Children complain that ketchup is touching their peas; they *never* complain that life is pointless. It occurs to me: life never had any meaning, because it's not a maths puzzle that can be solved. The secret of life is to play.

The problem with parenting manuals, I reckon, is that they tell you about the rules you impose on your children: Share, Wash Your Hands, Do Not Post Toast In The DVD Player. This is useful, but it doesn't make you eager about hanging out with your offspring. Which is bad, because kids copy their parents' moods, and their outlook on life. So it doesn't really matter what you feed them, or how early you start teaching them French. What matters is that you're actually happy yourself. My parents taught me a lot about how to read; they taught very little about how to be happy. I had to learn it, from my daughters.

So that's what this book is about. I tell you the parenting rules that I've learned by telling you the stories of how I learned them. I hope you'll pick up a few tips. Example: If you're really tired, take your top off, and invite your children to paint your back. You'll feel like you're being massaged by fairies. I'll tell you how we've coped with the big issues: sibling rivalry, choosing a school, getting them to eat *something* that's not a fish finger. I'll also tell you how I've coped with the big fears: Will I ever see my friends? Will I turn into my dad? Will we ever have sex again? So I hope you'll find that, in its own mad way, this book is curiously complete: it covers almost everything a modern parent might think about.

But, most of all, I hope the book does justice to the two small girls who inspired it. I hope that, like them, it's short, playful and shockingly intimate. I hope it makes you laugh. I hope it makes you cry. I hope it sprinkles glittery fairy dust on your life.

Dad Rules

*Me and Liv on the muddy beach, the day before the
incident I mention*

Rule 1: Avoid everything for as long as you can

July 1999, West Wittering
January 2000, Kentish Town

July 1999. We're on West Wittering beach. Kites are flying. Dogs are chasing balls. Liv squeezes my hand. 'Andrew,' she says, 'would you like to have children?' I know instantly this is a huge, historic moment. I know I must respond like a man. So I ignore her. Suddenly the wind is blasting sand against my legs. It's overcast. I walk off towards the car. She follows after me, saying: 'You can't ignore the subject forever, you know.' She's wrong about that. I reckon I can ignore it for two more years at least. The trouble is she keeps bringing it up ...

January 2000. It's a Saturday morning. I'm in heaven. The sun is streaming through the window. It's catching in the steam of my freshly brewed coffee. I'm sitting at the table, working on my Fantasy League Football team. I need a new midfielder, and I've still got 5.8 million quid. I could buy Darren Anderton for that; he's a bargain at 5.4. I'd practically be *making* money on Darren.

I hear a whimpering sound from upstairs. Liv is calling me. I hate it when she does that. If she needs to talk to me, why can't she visit me? I'm not a butler. I go upstairs, and find her sitting on the bed, staring tragically at the A4 box file that I've left on the desk.

'What's the *matter*?' I say. I'm instantly ready to help. I'll listen to her woes, I'll soothe her brow, I'll attack her enemies.

'Doesn't matter,' she says.

'NO! *No!* It *does* matter. Tell me.'

'It's . . . just . . .' She sniffs tragically. She stares at my dying bonsai tree.

'I just . . . I'd like to have *a baby, and* . . .'

At this point her voice goes squeaky. This is bad. She's raised the very worst subject she could raise, and she's raised it in the very worst way: she's actually crying. My every instinct is telling me to get the hell out of that room. I know I can't. I compromise by staring out of the window, at the small park we overlook.

A Staffordshire bull terrier is brazenly sniffing the arse of a red spaniel. Suddenly the terrier clambers on and starts thrusting. He looks cheerful. His tongue is hanging out like he's a grinning cockney scaffolder. He seems to be saying: 'Lovely-jubbley . . . you just stay where you are . . . I'll *sort you right out.*' Meanwhile the spaniel is pretending nothing is happening. She sniffs the air carefully, as if she's a critic whose job is assessing delicious smells. 'Oh yes . . .' she seems to be saying. 'There's a little bit of early dahlia . . . that's very fresh . . . and I can smell that those foxes have been at the bins . . . that's a bit more *urban.*'

'What are you looking at?' says Liv.

'Two dogs who're . . . having sex. Well . . . I think that's what they're doing. It's possible the one in front is blind. And the one behind is trying to push her round the park.'

Now Livy's blotchy tearful eyes are staring right at me. I just know something awful is going to happen.

'But aren't you going to SAY something?' says Liv.

'About what?'

'Having kids.'

'What do you want me to say?'

'Tell me the truth,' she says. Now that's never a good idea. 'Tell me what you *think* about having kids?'

I disappear into the most secret vault inside my head. I'm thinking: Well I definitely don't want kids. I don't think any men actually *want* kids. I've never met a broody man. I've got one friend, Dom, who had kids early, but Dom was adopted and spent his early drunken youth searching desperately for a family. Men never want kids now, because they know they can have them when they're ninety. They'll just have to be rich, or lucky, or good at golf. I've always assumed I'll be all of these things, as long as some woman doesn't stop me.

I consider what part of that I can actually say. I say nothing.

'Would you *like* to have kids?' she asks.

Oh God, how can I possibly know that? First I'd have to decide if I'm staying with Livy. Don't get me wrong. I *do* love her, but there's only one time when a man knows, for absolute certain, that he wants to stay with his woman for ever: when she's just chucked him. The rest of the time, he's not sure. I don't say that either.

'What is your *problem*?' she says. 'Why can't you talk about your feelings?'

I hate it when she says that. Loathe it. 'Oh ... OK. Right,' I say. 'Well ... my feelings are ... erm ... Terror.'

'Why?'

'I'm struggling to have a career as it is. I don't have any time to look after children.'

'But I'd do that.'

'Well ... would you? And I'm also quite *scared* of becoming a dad. Because I'm scared of turning into My Dad.'

'But your dad had five children!' she says.

'But he spent all his time avoiding them.'

'Oh, come on. Your dad's not so bad!'

I picture my dad. Big Dad, we call him. OK. He isn't so bad. He's funny. He gives a good hug. He can speak ten languages. If you want to know the Ancient Greek word for harp, he's your man. But he spent my entire childhood scowling at us from behind a pile of books about military history. If he did talk, he'd keep going for two hours. He'd give potted biographies of people he knew from the Bank of England. He'd speculate about careers he might have had if he hadn't made the mistake of having children. The implication was always clear: it was because of us that Dad's dreams were smashed. Liv's right. Big Dad isn't so bad, but he's the living embodiment of the man I'm trying not to be.

I don't say any of this. I just stare at the wall.

'Andrew,' says Liv. 'Forget your dad –'

'I'm trying to.'

'You don't think there are any dads who want to be dads?'

'No, I don't. That's why they have sheds. That's why they go out on pointless errands in the car. That's why they fish. Do you really think people *like* fishing? It involves staring at a pond for hours and hours, with the odd break where you get to torture a small creature.'

Livy starts weeping again. I realize, belatedly, that the jokes aren't working. When you're trying to comfort someone, you shouldn't use the words 'torture a small creature'.

'Sorry,' I say. Sorry is always a good start, I reckon. It's the equivalent of getting out the kitchen roll. You're preparing to start wiping up.

I put my hand on her shoulder. She shrugs it off, and her knuckles knock against my face. Suddenly I'm thinking: Oh God, she's actually *hitting* me now! I knew I shouldn't have talked about my feelings. Women never want you to talk about your feelings. They've got far too many of their own.

'Get out!' she says. 'GET OUT!!!'

'That's fine,' I say. And I mean it too. If it would get me out of that room, I would happily sign up for the French Foreign Legion.

Me and My Dad

and Tom Simpson (whose brother was with me at Christ Church) blah blah... and actually I COULD have joined the Grenadiers blah blah... I thought this was FUCKING self-indulgent...

please let me play ping-pong

Rule 2: Have sex with strangers

January 2000, ten minutes later, Kentish Town

Liv says she's going to see her sister. She goes out. Result. This means I can get on with some writing. I go upstairs and switch on. I'm working on a film script called *Sex with Strangers*. It's a political romantic comedy in the style of Charlie Kaufman. This is the story ...

Meg Ryan plays a presidential nominee, who finds her husband shagging a maid over the table. She can't stop and argue. She's on the way to a live presidential debate.

At the debate, the interviewer asks her: 'What are you going to do to preserve the family?'

And she loses it: 'Nothing,' she says. 'People have been going on for years about the family, but no one can do anything about it. Why? It's not like the Middle Ages, where you'd fall in love with the only person in the village who didn't have warts, and you'd love them till the day you died. Which was usually a week later. Now people live for years, and they fall in love, they have kids, but they want more, they fall in love again, have more kids, and eventually the kids grow up abandoned and angry and they beat the crap out of everyone before breeding themselves. Lust rules. The family is finished.'

'So ... what?' says the interviewer. 'Are you banning sex?'

'No. You can do it, but you shouldn't pretend it's about love. You should do it with someone new each time. In fact, it'll be illegal to sleep with someone twice. And the kids should be raised by the only people they can trust: the state.'

Her opponent looks at her: 'That's your policy? You're giving people endless sex. You've seriously underestimated the intelligence of the American people!'

Cut to:

Meg Ryan sweeping to a landslide election victory.

Cut to:

Four years later, the country is going well. The kids are all locked up. Old ladies feel safer. Everyone's healthier. And the economy is healthier too. Everyone's buying more. Shagging more. Working longer hours. The president is even more committed to her policy. As a routine courtesy, she always has sex with Olympic Gold athletes and any visiting dignitaries. The sex is broadcast on television. The voting public don't like it when she goes down on people. In the Second Act climax, Meg Ryan agrees to have sex with the president of China. While being skewered like a kebab, she secures a new trade agreement with China. Her approval ratings go through the roof.

Now that is only the beginning of the story. It's a romantic comedy, so obviously Meg Ryan does meet someone, a naïve monk played by Tobey Maguire, and she falls in love. So now she wants to sleep with him twice, and she sees that the whole policy is corrupt and evil. The story builds up to the ultimate feel-good ending, which I express with five words that I tell Livy confidently will earn me a one million pound script fee: *They fuck. The world celebrates.*

I bring up *Sex with Strangers* for three reasons.

1. I'm writing a script where adults have lives of boundless sex; kids are raised by the state: I have *issues* on the subject of kids. Fears.

7

2. You're probably thinking, *Sex with Strangers*
   starring Meg Ryan . . . Hmm . . . I don't recall
   ever seeing that film. And you'd be quite right.
   The film is never made. A producer called Robert
   Steapleton does eventually give me fourteen
   grand for the script, but that doesn't cover the
   two years I spend writing it. Translation: Liv is
   dealing with a man who earns fourteen grand for
   a two-year project, which has a deranged premise
   that only a mentalist would think up. This is not
   the man women dream of having babies with.
   And in my heart of hearts, I know the film won't
   work. The idea is not Swiftian – it's impractical.
   If it was funnier, someone would have given me
   more money for it. I'm not the dad I dreamed of
   being.

3. Robert Steapleton is one of my closest friends,
   and as I finish Draft Nine, he gets his girlfriend
   pregnant. She's a successful architect. She's kind,
   pretty, successful. She has lovely large breasts.
   When their baby is three months old, he walks
   out on her. At the same time as he walks out on
   my script. This is the world that Livy wants to
   bring children into.

Rule 3: Find the right girl

1991, Oxford
Winter 1999, Harlesden

I need to interrupt the story. I need to tell you where I meet Liv, and how.

I'm twenty. I'm at college. One evening, I'm watching a student fashion show. I become fascinated by one of the models. She looks shy and mysterious. She has shoulder-length brown hair, good cheekbones and one of those mouths that don't quite close so it looks like she's eternally ready for kissing. As she comes out, the room seems to go silent. I whisper, 'Who's that?' and someone says, 'That's Livy Lankester,' and just the name seems beautiful and enchanting. Two months later, I spend two minutes talking to her at a party, and it makes me feel confused and light-headed, and I have to go and sit down. Admittedly someone's just given me a blowback. I don't talk to her again before I leave college. I go home, and spend the summer at home. I spend the days painting our house with my brother. I spend the night dreaming I'm still at college, and I'm back with the beautiful girl that I only talked to once.

Three years later, I meet her in Russell Square in central London, and we stare into each other's eyes and we both forget what we were about to say. She tells me she's at the Tropical Disease Centre. 'Really?' I say. 'I'm often at the Tropical Disease Centre!' I did once have a friend who took me for lunch in the canteen. At this point I'd be willing to make another one. I write a letter there, suggesting we meet.

I get no response, but it doesn't put me off; I just know she's the right woman for me. So then whenever I'm in town I visit Russell Square for lunch. (There's a fine line between being very romantic, and being a stalker.) I eat a lot of sandwiches in the café. I see a lot of joggers going round and round. I don't see Livy. So instead I just look for her everywhere. I look for her in Russell Square; I look for her in Camden. One day I'm on a train that stops at Woking Station, and I can't stop myself: I get off and check if she's on the platform. She isn't.

Five more years pass, and life isn't going well. I'm an actor. I've got one of those CVs that sounds OK if you say it quickly enough, but the truth is I've been in movies that weren't distributed, and TV shows broadcast when there was something better on the other side. I usually arrive in programmes once they reach their last series. If you see me in a TV show, you know the show is doomed. As an actor, I've gone from hot to lukewarm. In terms of hotness, my career is like one of those tepid baths that bring you no pleasure, but you're too demoralized to get out, so you lie there vainly hoping the boiler will heat up.

I own a one-bedroom flat in Harlesden, a place which is the geographical equivalent of a lukewarm scummy bath floating with pubic hairs. I'm so poor that, when I'm walking to the shop for my milk, I scour the gutters for extra 2p pieces. I hardly even remember what Livy looks like any more, but know it's a tiny bit like Kate Beckinsale. Once a week, my friend David Walliams takes me to the theatre, and I always say: 'I'll get the drinks.' I put my card in the wall, it says: 'Your request has been denied.' David always says: 'Don't worry. I'll get the drinks.' And I feel touched by his tenderness, but stiff with a sense of failure. I don't believe in anything. David's got a partnership with this guy called Matt, who's really sweet, but they've just had yet another sitcom rejected by the BBC. I don't think their work together is gelling. I advise them both to split up.

One day, David invites me to his birthday party, to which he's wearing a full-length sequin dress. He introduces me to Kate Beckinsale. She says: 'You're getting lovely reviews at the moment.' Now it's been two years since I was in anything, and I've never had lovely reviews. I acted in the first Royal Court production of *Shopping and Fucking*. Critics raved about the text; they applauded the furniture; not one of them mentioned my performance. My problem is: I don't know who I am. I figure that Kate Beckinsale is offering me an opportunity to find out. If I know who I'm *like*, that could help. I say: 'Kate, *who* do you think that I am?'

She immediately walks off.

I think what's the point of this? And I leave the party, and bump into Eleanor, who I know to be Livy's friend. I get her address. I write Liv a letter, via Eleanor, in which I declare my feelings in the grand Victorian manner. I begin: 'You've got to put a name to the face you're looking for in a crowd, and for me it's always been yours.'

I get no reply.

Five months later, I am in my flat. I've just cycled through a rainstorm, and I'm wringing my wet socks into the kitchen sink. The phone rings. I run to the living room. 'Hi,' says a voice, which sounds pure and beautiful like fresh mountain water. 'It's Livy. I got your letter.'

I pull the phone out of the wall. Trembling, I get the plug back in. She's still talking. She's saying she once sent me a Valentine card, when we were at college, but sent it to the wrong Andrew. She says she never went to the Tropical Disease Centre, she just thought it sounded interesting and romantic. (Who the hell is turned on by malaria?) She's just come back from the Ukraine. She's been living in Karkov, helping people set up new businesses. She says she's having a party the next day.

The next day, I go to Livy's party. I walk in. I see Livy. She doesn't look like Kate Beckinsale. She looks skinnier than I remember. She's no longer a luscious student; she's a professional woman. I notice everyone is looking at me and whispering. I realize that almost everyone has read my letter. I feel uneasy. I go home before the end of the party, leaving Livy with an annoying banker who seems intent on shagging her.

She calls a couple of days later. She didn't shag the banker. She suggests a date. A week later, we're sitting on the bottom stair of the World's End Pub in Camden Town, and we're holding hands.

Three months later, she asks me to rent out my Harlesden flat. I lend it to my friend, Nick Rowe, who's just left his girlfriend because she wanted to get serious. I move in with Liv.

You see why I have to say all that. It isn't just *anyone* who is proposing having kids with me. It is my Fantasy Woman. This is the person who is watching me being dragged towards parenthood, like a stubborn dog being dragged towards his bath.

man, being dragged towards parenthood

Rule 4: Don't expect anyone to share in your happiness

February 2000, London, East End

Admittedly, Livy does things that no woman would ever do in a fantasy. In the morning she eats cereal in bed, so she wakes me with the chink of spoon on bowl, and the sound of a bolus of food being swallowed. She uses my razors on her underarms. She says: 'Let's talk about money.' But she also does things that are endearing and surprising. She's just got a new job at the Cabinet Office, and she comes home with hilarious stories about drunk civil servants, and vain cabinet ministers. I don't know what her work is exactly. I like to picture her as a sort of post-feminist Miss Money-penny, all pert and sexy and full of strange plans.

In our first summer together, she wants to take me to the Ukraine, because she wants to see Yalta, where Chekhov spent his summers. In Yalta, she wants to go to the circus, because she loves clowns. When we reach the circus, we find out it's closed, since the clown is getting married. Livy says: 'Let's tell him we've come from England to pay homage to the famous clown. Let's give him a wedding present. Let's peek at the big top. Then we'll go.' So we go off and find a big wooden spoon, and some flowers, and a shopkeeper who teaches us a little speech for the clown. We return to the circus, and are ushered into the middle of the big top. The clown is wearing his wife's flowery veil. We make our speech. We bow. We give our gifts. The whole circus cheers. We are embraced like long-lost friends. The flowers are fed to the crocodiles. The wooden spoon is given to the parrots as a new perch. The clown shows Liv a horse, which is, he assures her, 'worth ten million dollars'.

'But why?' says Liv. 'Why is he worth ten million dollars?'

'Because he is a *dancing* horse,' says the clown. 'He dances to rock. To disco. He can even dance to opera. Here, you must try.'

I'm standing on a table with a contortionist, feeding a baby monkey from a little bottle. Liv enters the big top, sitting on the dancing horse, which is dancing to, of all things, the ELO's 'Last Train to London', which is pretty much my favourite song. Jeff Lynne is singing: 'There was magic in the air, it was so right!' The dancing horse is pirouetting. Liv is waving proudly. 'Darling!' she shouts. 'I think we're in!'

Soon after returning home, we go to the East End to fetch our friend Kara, who's an impoverished writer. Kara is renting a room from Roy and Emma Ashford, who, it turns out, have just had a baby – Theo Ashford. As soon as I enter the house, I notice something unpleasantly weird about the atmosphere. We're shown into the kitchen where there's a crowd of murmuring people, including Roy who is holding his new baby. He looks like a recently converted Christian. He is grinning like a fool, and he's whispering. It's like he's trying to be extra soft, and I find this a bit annoying, and a bit gay.

I then feel immeasurably distant from Liv as she peers at the baby and exclaims: '*Oh, he's beautiful!*' I find it shocking just how ugly little Theo Ashford actually is. He has weird red blotchy skin, which is flaky round the eyes. He looks like a monkey that's been peeled. I say, 'He's lovely,' and go off to another room. I'm hoping I won't have to see anyone else before we can leave.

In the living room, I find an *Independent*, and I read about an upcoming Manchester United European tie. I discover that in the forthcoming match Alex Ferguson thinks the battle will be won in midfield. I find this information reassuring.

But then another man comes in pushing a buggy with a sleeping boy in it. The man doesn't give his name. He's grinning too. Everyone is smiling in this house. It's like being in the headquarters of a cult. He says: 'This little feller can walk now ... I can hardly believe it.' I want to say: 'Listen, almost everyone in the world can walk! If you want to impress me, tell me he can *fly*! Tell me that little monkey got out of his pushchair and soared several hundred metres above Hackney!'

I say nothing.

Soon we are able to escape that horrible house, and I feel liberated. Livy and Kara are in high spirits too. Liv is wearing my trilby hat, and she's laughing, which I always find very attractive. At one point she takes Kara's arm, and they skip down the street together. I think: I *could* have kids with her, but not yet. *Definitely* not yet. And only if she stops eating cereal in bed.

Rule 5: Don't get wrecked every night (do it in the daytime)

1994, Bow, East London

The only time I ever take crack, I'm living in Bow, in the East End. Our street is where the council houses all the single mums, so the place is filled with mums who are looking for lovers, and kids who are looking for dads. The dads do turn up every now and again, and the mums snap instantly into action: the police are called. In the East End, they always say, 'Blood's thicker than water,' which is true, especially if the blood is congealed on the pavement. They love proverbs in the East End. They love to say: 'It's not what you know, it's who you know,' as if the only reason they're unemployed is they haven't met Richard Branson down the market.

Three months after moving in, I get my first job as an actor. I'm a baddie in *The Bill*. Actors always scorn *The Bill*, but cockneys don't. In the first ad break, the doorbell rings and there're ten kids crammed into the doorway. They cheer.

'You hit the Old Bill!' shouts a little boy.

'You called him a wanker!' shouts a little girl.

'Quick!' I say. 'The adverts are finishing. We've got to get back!'

They all run off.

The next day, I'm walking back from the market with Trisha, who's twenty-four, the same age as me, and she's sexy in a skinny, missing-half-her-teeth sort of way. She's my best friend in the area. She's recently out of prison. She had a smack/crack habit for five years; she had multiple convictions for armed robbery; she had a little girl called Meghan who's now four. So she's trying to get clean, and has managed it for six months.

Trish disappears. She comes back with some white rocks.

'Oh, Trish,' I say, 'are you sure about this? I don't want you to take it.'

'I've got it now, Andrew,' she says, 'I've got to have it.'

'Give me half then,' I say. 'I don't want you having too much.'

We go up to her mum's flat, which smells of bleach. Trish puts foil over a cup, she mixes the crack with some fag ash, and then we inhale it. I'm told you can get instantly addicted to crack. I'm instantly disgusted. It's like having a line of coke, while sucking on an ash tray.

While doing it, I say: 'So why did you have Meghan?'

'I love Meghan,' she says. 'I want to get clean for her.'

'She's a lovely girl. But why did you have her?'

'I didn't think too much,' she says. 'But I just . . . sort of . . . had had enough of going out and getting wrecked every night.'

After this incident, I never take crack again, but I often ask people the same question: 'Why did you want to have kids?' It's amazing how often I get that answer: 'I was tired of getting wrecked every night.' These people don't want children. They want rehab. They are so determined to avoid hangovers they're prepared to breed. They are not realizing that, if they do have kids, the sofa will be covered in Lego, the toilet will be covered in pee and the whole world will feel like a hangover. But a small part of me still envies Trish. I think *way* too much.

Crack: not as much fun as you might think

this is a spikey prince
He's sad because he could
find no princesses to marry.

Rule 6: Commit to something, or you end up with nothing

January 2001, Bayswater and Kentish Town

Seven years on. Liv and I have gone to a party. Liv loves going to parties. She loves arriving at them, and seeing the set-up – the lights, the people, the food – then she likes to go. She's too impatient to linger. She's in the front room, dancing. I'm on the balcony, and I'm chatting to this guy called Graham who's shagging my friend Vicky. He is a slightly successful DJ, who runs his own voice-over company. He's wearing a leather jacket, and his breath smells of fags and garlic tablets. He's fifty-six. Vicky told me. She also told me he's scared of commitment. Graham doesn't know who I am. He also doesn't know I'm Vicky's spy.

I say to him: 'Would you like to have children?'

'One day,' he says.

'But when?' I say.

'Not yet. I don't wanna be held down.'

I have a brief desire to hold him down and punch him. Vicky is thirty-six, and wants children. Graham doesn't realize that, for Vicky, he's wasting vital months.

'But why?' I say.

'I wanna be free,' says Graham. 'I like to be able to take off whenever I want.'

Now I want to see him take off from the balcony. I'd like to see him plunging through the conservatory downstairs. Then Liv arrives and tells me she wants to go. I'm amazed she's lasted this long. We've been at the party ninety minutes at least.

In the car, I tell her about the conversation, then immediately regret it. I know she's going to say: 'Do *you* want to have kids?' But she doesn't. She changes the subject. She asks if we could get a lodger. I immediately agree. It'll draw attention away from the fact I'm earning nothing. Then Liv asks me something unexpected. She says: 'Do you want to get a dog?'

I see instantly what's happening: Liv knows that I'm terrified of commitment and responsibility. She's suggesting a dog, as a sort of warm up. I'm about to say: 'Not yet,' but then I realize that's what Graham said. I also realize I'm going to have to compromise somewhere or she'll leave me. Besides, I like dogs. If we get a dog, I say, it should be a big one, a lurcher, or a Great Dane. She says it should be a small one that can fit in the car.

A week later, we get a border terrier. She is the size of an adult cat, but with all the yap of a larger animal. She has a bushy moustache and eyebrows so she looks like a World War One general. We discuss names. I hate poncy names that I wouldn't want to shout in the park: '*Thomasina* ... leave the sandwich ALONE!' I hate the cute names that posh people always give their dogs: George, Milly, Biscuit. I want to call the dog Raff. That sounds like a name a dog would call herself. Liv agrees. She's clever. She's saving herself for bigger arguments.

Before long I am happily leaving parties saying: 'I've got to let the dog out.' I am going running with Raff, and we're both fit and healthy. Now Livy starts getting really sexy. This puts me on my guard. I've seen what happens. The average couple conceive three months after purchasing the dog.

One night, we invite Jed over. He's got kids, but he isn't dead. In fact, he has a lot of fun. OK, he doesn't have any money, but he has fun. I ask him if he ever regrets it.

He says: 'In divorces, you never hear of people who sue so they *don't* have custody – "Your honour, I'm not bloody looking after them. They've ruined my life enough!"'

He asks me what sort of kids I think I'll have. Suddenly I imagine them hiding in cupboards calling to me: 'Daddy? Daddy? Let me out. I want to meet you. I want to start playing.' Suddenly I feel tender towards these unborn children. This thought is so different from my normal fearful thoughts. It's like the sound of a piano, just audible above the pneumatic drill.

Also, Jed leaves a present, *Sperm Wars*, which I read right away. It argues that everything human beings do they do it in order to reproduce. If a man masturbates in the middle of the afternoon, it's because he's unconsciously making sure that, come evening time, his sperm will be fresh. If a woman has a mid-morning shag with the postman, it's because she knows she's fertile; she knows she's found a fertile man; she cannot resist. I learn that one in ten children are not fathered by the person they call Dad. (That means there's a one in ten chance that my mum's a slag.) I realize I have to get on with it. Any second now, Livy could be meeting a postman. She's meeting the lodger every day.

I also learn that a man produces ten million sperm a day: each man is like a mad racehorse trainer who's been breeding horses for a horse race that has never happened. And suddenly I feel an instinctive love for those tiny horses, just like we feel love for that horse that we see in the Grand National, who loses his rider, *but carries on anyway*. And I feel particular love for that horse: the one that will leap the final barrier and win the race and come crashing into the gigantic

23

paddock that is the egg. I see that the horse does have a jockey, and it's a little tiny me.

I can't say for sure I'm thinking all that the moment before conception. I imagine I'm thinking what any man is thinking before he conceives a new life. I'm thinking: Just look at her breasts. Just look at them. I'm going to touch them. And I'm going to pretend we're under some coats at a party . . .

the horse does have a jockey and
it's a little tiny me

Rule 7: Take the news like a man

March 2001, Kentish Town

I'm evasive. I don't like hearing about things I don't understand. I screen out anything that's connected with Science
and Technology. It confuses and frightens me. If someone
discusses it, I'll disappear to my Safe Place for a moment.
I'll hide away in the darkness, like a scared woodland
animal, and I'll read about football until I feel safe. I do have
knowledge, and I have expertise, but only on three different
subjects: football, fairy stories and the Electric Light
Orchestra. People say knowledge is power, but that's not
true if that knowledge is about the Electric Light Orchestra.
One thing I really don't understand is pregnancy. I don't
understand how sperms are alive, but you can freeze them. I
don't understand how you can have two cells that become
four cells that become someone who wipes jam on your
CDs.

I'm in the kitchen. It's a Tuesday evening. Liv comes towards me brandishing a plastic thing.

'Look,' she says, smiling. 'I've just peed on this.'

I'm thinking: If this is important, why have you peed on it?

'There's a blue mark,' she says.

'Great,' I say.

'I'm pregnant.'

'OK,' I say. But I'm not there any more. I'm hiding away in my hole. I'm clutching little pieces of leaf, and I'm sniffing them.

Rule 8: Keep it a secret

Spring 2001, Kentish Town and A Big House in Yorkshire

'Now listen,' says Liv, conspiratorially, 'you're NOT allowed to tell anyone about this for three months.'

I'm thinking: My friends are men. They want my opinions about playing Beckham out of position; they don't want to hear about babies. But Liv's lady friends all work out the secret anyway, the very first time she puts her hand over the glass, and says: 'No wine for me. I'm cutting back.' Women are like wolves. They can smell fresh babies.

The three months are up on a weekend when we're invited to stay at the house of Jenny, who I met twelve years ago under a table at a party. Jenny is a delightful human being who loves art and laughing and falling in love with bold, free-thinking, artistic men. Jenny's problem is that bold, free-thinking artists are usually terrified of long-term, serious relationships. Her other problem is that her favourite seduction technique is sitting her man down for a Serious Chat about where things are going. Doubtless she thinks I'm a sexist pig, but I think she'd do better to try a more traditional technique: she should get drunk and wear stockings. Jenny is just back from Alaska, where she met up with a gaunt artist, who'd just cycled, solo, across Canada, filming himself as he went. Now I don't know the man, but I'm guessing that he cycled solo, across Canada, after some woman tried to make him have a Serious Chat about their relationship. I'm also guessing the guy isn't enamoured with domesticity, or company. I'm wondering who Jenny will go for next ... A gay man who hates children? A former murderer, who swears he's now definitely off the smack?

In the meantime, I'm very happy to have Jenny back. Her parents are old-fashioned Bohemians and have a big house filled with paintings, and dog hair, and old bedspreads that smell of mothballs. It's the most welcoming place in England. For the weekend, it's filled with foppish young men, and well-bred ladies who all have men's names like Georgie, or Charlie, or Alex, or Keith. (Not Keith, I made that one up.) At dinner, there's a lull in the conversation, and then Liv says: 'By the way, we've got some news ...' There's an expectant silence. Oh no, I'm thinking. We don't even know these people. They may not like babies. They may not like us. They're all in their mid-twenties, which, for posh people, is way too early for kids. And then Liv makes it worse. She says: 'You tell them, Andrew.'

That's a bad trick. It's not like this is a story where I want to say the punchline. I get a hot, flushed feeling, like you get when you walk into a shop with your hot winter's clothing.

'Yes,' I say, smiling bravely. 'We're ... er ... we're having a baby.'

A little pause.

Then a bloke called Hugo says: 'Man ... that's *awesome*.' A girl called Philly comes over and says: 'Ohhhhhh, that's *sooooooo* sweet. You're having a lickle baby.' I realize that's the thing I most hate about babies. All that skwummy-wummy shloopy-woopy lickle baby thing. But I know it would be rude to punch Philly in the face.

Jenny says to me: 'So you're going to be a dad?'

'Yes.'

'Are you going to be there at the birth?'

'Yes.'

'Aren't you … aren't you a bit worried that, if you see that, it might put you off sex?'

'Jenny,' I say, 'when Liv is giving birth, I really don't think I'm gonna want to … have sex with her. Imagine if the midwife came in, to find me cheerfully penetrating. "Stay in there, little feller … Daddy's coming in!"'

Jenny says: 'That's not what I mean, and you know it.'

Whatever, the secret is out. People keep congratulating me, which seems strange. No one congratulated me when I first had sex. I was dying for praise then. I gave that girl six seconds of sheer pleasure.

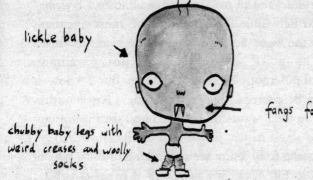

lickle baby

fangs for chewing breasts

chubby baby legs with weird creases and woolly socks

Rule 9: Spoil the surprise

Summer 2001, Kentish Town
Autumn 2001, Stoke Newington

Livy doesn't want to find out the sex of the baby. She thinks it'll 'spoil the surprise'. I tell her: 'Darling, a small person's head is going to appear out of you, like a big pink egg. As if that weren't surprising enough!' I want to find out the sex, because we're having a nightmare thinking up the names.

We go and have a scan. The nurse points to a monitor that, occasionally, shows a picture of a squirming tadpole.

'Your baby is beautiful,' says the nurse.

I'm thinking she has a very weird sense of beauty. Does she have kids with giant heads, and tails that flip around on the sofa? I don't want an assessment on our child's beauty. I just want to know the sex. I ask.

'Well, I can't see any male genitals,' she says. 'But I'm not certain we'd see them.'

'How dare you?' I want to say. 'If my child was a boy, his genitals would be visible from space.' The nurse is pretty sure we're having a girl. I ask her if everyone wants to know the sex.

'Everyone is different,' she says.

People may be different, but, over the next few months, I find that everyone wants to (1) pat Livy's stomach, and (2) give advice about names, in which they all compete to be as dirty as possible. I tell Jenny we're thinking of Elva, which means a Female Elf. 'Yes,' she says, 'but it suggests vulva.'

I tell my mum we're thinking of calling her Lupa, which means Wolf-girl. 'No,' she says, 'people will call her Loo. Or perhaps Toilet.' I tell my brother we're thinking of Grace. He says: '*MAN*, you can't call her Grace! Remember that girl at school who used to charge five p for showing people her pants? She was called Grace. She died early.'

We go to the Natural Birth Clinic in Tufnell Park to meet a woman called Amber who's got hennaed hair, and breath that smells of raw onion. She shows me how to massage the lady in labour, by massaging just above the kidneys. She tells Liv that the important thing during labour is to breathe. That's a relief to me. I've been worrying that Liv might try holding her breath throughout the whole ordeal. She tells us the important thing when giving birth is to lean forward. 'Squat,' says Amber, demonstrating, 'be like an animal.' She tells us that doctors are all trying to get you to lie back and take drugs. I'm thinking surely that's not doctors; it's pimps. She says that if you have one intervention – drugs – you're likely to need more – e.g. Caesarean. That's a principle any modern parent can grasp. If you take a sleeping pill, you'll need coffee in the morning; if you take coke, you'll need a valium; if you're waking at 6 a.m. every morning to go to work, you're going to need bloody long holidays.

We go to the NHS pre-natal, where a midwife enthusiastically lists the drug options: gas-and-air – 'laughing gas' – which I know all about, cos I had it at a Grateful Dead concert. Admittedly I wasn't giving birth at the time. As far as I'm aware.

'Any questions?' asks the midwife.

'Yes!' I say. 'We'd like to give birth . . . well Livy would . . . leaning forward. Squatting. Is that OK?'

'That's absolutely fine. Just tell your midwife.'

31

I expected more of a fight. 'But ... does that make it easier?' I ask.

'Everyone is different,' says the midwife. I'm sensing that health-care professionals always say that. It's the code. If any of them break it, their houses are picketed by midwives and nannies, who stand around sullenly, holding placards and packets of wet wipes.

Liv's girlfriends come round in a great posse of perfume and pashminas. They drink prodigious quantities of white wine in the kitchen, and they repeat their Birth Stories like they're Vietnam Vets going over their campaigns.

'I was in labour for two days,' says the competitive friend who has the amazing career. 'And I didn't even have an aspirin.'

'All my doctors were incompetent,' says the one who drives a Volvo. 'The anaesthetist was drunk ... The registrar was only twenty; he looked like he was *tripping* at the time. So they cut me open, and they gave me a Caesarean, through my back ... Well, it felt like that.'

'The important thing is to relax,' says the third, a tense interior designer who's on beta-blockers. 'I found the whole experience *really* moving and lovely. The important thing is to enjoy it.'

The result of all this is Liv makes a decision: she will out-do all her friends. She will have no drugs. My job is to massage, play gentle classical music and to back up all her decisions.

I promise to do that, but Liv does not relax. In the seventh month, she wakes me up, on several occasions, to say: 'We need to talk about money.' I don't wake up for sex. I definitely don't want to wake up for a financial assessment. The first couple of times, I say petulantly: 'I AM earning money!' I am actually going through a brief bout of professional success. Last summer I did a comedy show that got nominated for the Perrier Award. I still haven't earned any money, but I'm having some very high-level meetings. I'm writing some of the best material that's ever filled a drawer. I've also got a part-time BBC job editing sit-com scripts. I've still got my flat in Harlesden, and some poor bastard is renting it. I'm a landlord. I tell all this to Liv, although she knows it. She says: 'But how do we KNOW you're always going to have ENOUGH money?' She doesn't relax.

I do a live comedy show at Edinburgh in front of two hundred people where I interview Tony Parsons for my Radio 4 show, *Storyman*. His wife's pregnant, and he's saying reasonably: 'Pregnancy is like flying. The excitement is all at the beginning and the end. The rest is just plain sailing.' I suddenly lose it, and start ranting: 'It is for YOU, Tony, cos you're rich. My girlfriend is waking me up at 2 a.m., and saying to me: "We need to move to Hampstead where it's safe ... but we don't have *money* to move to Hampstead ... OH, God, please cut off your toenails; I NEED to eat something CRUNCHY with calcium in it!" Pregnancy is like flying, Tony, in that it involves terror. And weird food. And being stuck next to someone who keeps wanting to puke. If you're flying like that, you're going EasyJet.'

This is a good routine, but you're not supposed to rant when you're interviewing someone. It doesn't make them forthcoming. It scares them. And it doesn't solve my problems at home. And it doesn't stop the avalanche of advice.

Everyone's telling me how women eat strange things in pregnancy, but no one tells me about a far more worrying phenomenon: women move house; women knock through walls; women redecorate. Liv decides our Kentish Town flat won't be big enough, and we buy and sell and move to a larger, cheaper house in Stoke Newington with a month to go before birth. She sacks the decorators and takes over. A week to go, she's urgently painting, but not using the gloss paint, which, she knows, is bad for babies. She's working at a phenomenal speed. I realize you could have a decorating company staffed entirely by pregnant women. Admittedly, it would be an ordeal to feed them. At lunchtime they'd all be lying about like chubby damsels-in-distress saying: 'Just one thing . . . We need muesli, with crunchy apple in it, and please add some DICED SNAIL SHELLS.' If you refused, they'd all cry. So the catering would be a nightmare. But God they'd work fast.

And everyone's telling me to relax, but no one's telling that to Livy. In the ninth month, she sleeps about two hours a night. I challenge her on this. She says: 'Well, I'm scared that, if I go to sleep, the baby will just . . . pop out. And then you'll have to deal with it.' People say you can't sleep when you've got babies, but I thought that while they were still inside the womb we'd be OK.

I'm upstairs one Friday afternoon, and Livy calls to me. She's sitting on the edge of the bath. 'My waters have broken,' she says, and she immediately gets her bag and goes to the car. She packed the bag a night ago. She's even put in four babygros and some nappies. She's so ready. And so we set off together in the car to the Elizabeth Garrett Anderson Hospital in Central London.

It's a big ramshackle building with high ceilings and plastic floors and a scrum of people – babies, toddlers, grannies, dads, nurses. It feels like a refugee camp. Previously, I've been an ardent leftie about hospitals. My view has been: 'NHS doctors have the same experience as private ones, just different golf clubs.' Now I see why people spend five grand at the Portland. It's to avoid this moment.

We queue for ages at reception. The receptionist has blonde hair and a mean mouth. I say:

'We're having a baby.'

She doesn't congratulate us. She says: 'Has your labour started?'

'Yes,' says Liv. 'My waters broke an hour ago.'

'But has your labour started? Your contractions?'

'Er . . . no.'

'Then you must go home.'

'What?' I say.

'How long from waters breaking to contractions starting?' I ask.

'Everyone is different.'

And suddenly I can't take it any more. 'But please give us an *average*!' I say. 'Give us an *estimate*!'

'Everyone is different,' she says again, and I feel so desperate I want to stand on the desk and start shouting: 'Can someone find me a MAN who can give an answer to a question? If I ask a plumber how long it takes to fit a pipe, he takes a guess. It may be a lie! But at least it's something! Everyone is NOT different! Everyone is saying the same stupid bloody thing and I'm going to fight someone!' But I have learned that, around women, you must never show your feelings, and there's no more female place than a maternity wing.

So we drive home. And that's the end of the pregnancy experience. A time during which I learn that almost all advice is unhelpful; it would be better just to go with your instinct. I figure out one bit of advice, which no one tells me. You could make tea towels out of this one:

PREGNANCY
is Nature's Way
of telling a lady
she's driving home

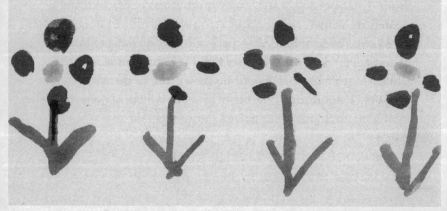

Rule 10: Shut the doors. Disconnect the phone. The party is here

5–7 January 2002, Stoke Newington and Elizabeth Garrett Anderson Hospital

The whole atmosphere calms. I mean, what else am I supposed to be doing for the weekend? I don't need to drive to Daventry for a comedy gig. I don't need to go out and see friends. It's simple. It's easy. I should be nowhere but here. I must look after my girlfriend as we both wait for her labour to start. We wait all Friday night. All Saturday. Saturday night. On Sunday, it's now two days since the waters broke. 'We've all been here,' I say, speaking to the bump, 'we've let the plug out, and the bath has emptied, and we're lying on the floor of an empty tub like a big pink slug. It's not nice to get out, but you must.' And I tell Liv how I once visited my friend Helen and I induced labour by sharing a tub of chicken korma. Over that weekend, Liv keeps ordering curries. I eat most of them.

But nothing happens. On Sunday evening, we're eating more curry and I'm telling Liv my main concern about birth. I was born at home, and my mum has never been able to tell me what was the exact time of birth. This means I've never been able to do a proper horoscope chart, which is something I've fiercely resented. I'm determined, for our child, to get the *exact* time. She makes a funny face.

'What's the matter?'

'Either that was a contraction,' she says, 'or my womb's just got cramp.'

We return to the Elizabeth Garrett Anderson Hospital. It no longer feels like a refugee camp. It feels cool and ramshackle. The same girl is sitting in reception.

'Either my wife is having contractions,' I say, looming over her meaningfully, 'or her womb's got cramp.'

These are the magic words.

'All right,' she says, 'you sit right there, and we'll get a room ready for you.'

We go and sit in the waiting room. There's a Polish couple, who've got a toddler, and a Philippine couple, who've brought parents. When the Poles leave to go to their room, we say: 'Good luck,' and they thank us. I'm tempted to go over and hug them, but I've eaten such a vast quantity of curry I fear I'd unleash a massive fart. Liv touches her stomach.

'Is that a contraction?' I say.

'Oh yes,' she says. 'I'm definitely having them now. I've been feeling them regularly for about half an hour now.'

'What? You mean ... It's started ... it's definitely started?'

'Yes. It's started.'

'Great,' I say.

And I really mean it. It feels like the beginning of an adventure. Like we're planning to go out to a club for the night. We've taken our Es. Things haven't started going too weird yet, but they will. We don't care. We're coming up. We're OK. But of course I feel that. I'm not the one who's going to feel like they're shitting out a hedgehog. Liv is going to be running the marathon. I'll be riding in the car eating pizza.

We go into our room where there's a Nigerian lady called Grace waiting for us. Grace has large breasts and calm ways.

I set about, as discussed, putting on soothing music. Grace applauds this. 'Good boy,' she says, and it's a difficult thing to stop hugging her.

Livy has contractions. She breathes, like Amber advised, she gyrates her hips. 'Good girl,' says Grace. I adjust the music, I massage the spot. 'Good boy,' says Grace.

At midnight, Liv's still not had an aspirin. If only her friends could see her now. She has another contraction. I adjust the music. I touch the spot. Liv says: *'Will you turn off that fucking music? And Stop Fucking Touching Me.'* Suddenly she's shouting like a crack addict: *'Can I have the drugs? Can I just have the bloody drugs?'* And I want to say something about intervention, but I know my job is to back her up. And I will. You don't mess with a woman in labour. Even if she decides she wants to *eat* the baby, I'll back her up.

The storm passes. Liv immediately asks for the evil epidural. Grace says: 'That's just fine. We'll make it so it wears off enough when it's time to push.' The epidural is fitted. Liv relaxes. She says: 'Epidurals are *fantastic*. Why didn't I do this earlier?'

But then more hours have passed, and it's five in the morning. Three doctors arrive. All three of them insert their hands into Livy, one by one, and they feel around. Meanwhile they look at the ceiling, and make worried faces. I don't know what face you should have when you're wearing a woman as a glove, but I'm sure it's not that one. They send for the consultant. He can't come. That's not reassuring. The doctors keep coming, and going, and they're putting their hand into Livy, as if she were a Lucky Dip, and she is exhausted. I can't imagine how she's going to be able to push this baby out. Let alone look after it for the next twenty years. Finally they tell us what the matter is. The baby has been refusing to come out for three days, but now she *is* coming; she's tried to push her way out with her hand, and that's got her stuck.

Grace says: 'Don't worry. Theatre starts at nine. We'll wait till then.' Liv is happy with that. Grace is happy with that. I'm furious. If the doctors yank the baby out, then how is that supposed to affect the chart? It'll render it meaningless. But then I look at my girlfriend, and I'm not worried about the baby. I'm worried about Liv. I know how, in the year 1700, one in thirteen women died during childbirth. It was not the delivery that did for them. It was the haemorrhage afterwards.

But then we're given blue coats, and at 9 a.m. we're swooped downstairs to the delivery theatre, and there're about ten doctors in there. Everyone's got on their blue coats, just like mine. I feel good. I used to be in the medical programme *Cardiac Arrest*, and I feel I know where I am. Any second the cameras will roll, Helen Baxendale will do ballet just out of shot and everything will be normal. It's calm in the theatre. The radio is playing. To the doctors, it's a normal Monday morning at work. But I'm worried about Liv. I'm holding her hand, and she looks very suffering, and then suddenly one of the doctors is brandishing a ventouse – one of those things that looks like a sink-plunger – and he's thrusting it into Liv like her pipes are blocked with potato peel. I turn away to check the clock. It's 9.13 a.m. Then I just look at Liv, and she looks beautiful, and suddenly her eyes relax, like she's OK, and someone says: 'Right. That's done.' And I kiss Liv, and then someone says: 'Would you like to come and cut the cord?' I want to say 'I *really* wouldn't!' but that's not the right thing to say, so the next thing I know I'm cutting at this thing that looks like a long sausage filled with black pudding, and then they're wrapping the baby tightly, and they're giving her to me, and I take her ever so gently to the edge of the room, and I can hear a tiny, tiny voice going 'ooo ooo' like a little scared mouse as if she's saying, 'Daddy ... Daddy ... will I be all right?' and I whisper to her, 'Darling. It's OK. I'll look after you,' and suddenly my legs are twitching like I'm drunk, and I'm weeping uncontrollably.

*My daughter, four days
old, being held by my friend
the actor Nick Rowe*

Rule 11: Get help

7–9 January 2002, Hospital/Hoxton/
Stoke Newington

After a few hours, it's time for me to leave. We're pretty sure we're going to call the baby Grace, but we have forty-two days to register her name, so there's no hurry. As I drive home, I'm spaced out. I suddenly find myself outside my friend Phil's house. I buzz up to his flat. He says: '*Andrew* ... come up!' I enter, and he says: 'So what have you been doing?'

I say: 'I've just come back from the hospital. Liv's just given birth.'

But of course I've made a mistake talking to a boy, not a girl. Phil says: 'Congratulations ... And what else is going on?'

I return to the hospital next day. Liv and I keep looking at Grace. She seems so remarkably beautiful. Yes, the delivery gave her a big red birthmark on her forehead, but she's lovely. Also the ventouse means that the top of her head is pointed like a Smurf's, but you've never seen a more enchanting Smurf.

Then the doctors tell me I should drive her home. That scares me. I have driven before, but now it feels like it's the first time. Suddenly everything feels like it's the first time. It seems amazing that someone would trust me with a vehicle, with a young child. I'm not ready for this. I'm not ready for anything. I wonder if we should give the baby back to the nice nurses. I'll just tell them: 'Everyone is different.

Some people can be parents. Some can't.' And then I'll run off like Robert Steapleton.

In the car, on the way home, Liv gives me the next plan. 'Right,' she says, 'no visitors allowed.' What she means is: she doesn't want my mum running the show. My mum is called Val, but we call her SuperVal, because she likes Supervising. If you're loading the dishwasher, she lingers in the background saying: 'Did you *want* to put the glasses there?' She raised five children of her own, and at the same time she ran a playschool where I used to work in my holidays. It was in Luxembourg, and was filled with international children. My mum spoke to everyone in her mad Euro language: 'Yuki ... *nein* ... **right**, you're going in the corner. *Allez-vite. Aber schnell.*' My mum is great at talking to kids. She's less good at talking to adults. She overuses the phrase: 'It's always the way!' She's one of those people who can never leave a room. We've invented a phrase – to Val your exit – to describe the way my mum lingers at doors saying: 'Goodbye ... We'll call you next week ... and send my love to Roger ... and as I say the dinner was *lovely* ...' She also has superhuman levels of stamina, and cheerfulness, and generosity. She adopts cancerous neighbours, and she nurses them. And I tell you, if you've got to have cancer, my mother is an excellent person to do it near. She gives good service. My dad takes full advantage. For the last twenty years, he's been suffering from numerous life-threatening medical conditions. He's finally attained Nirvana: he's eighteen stone, and got thirty per cent lung capacity, and a bad back. This allows him to lie on the sofa while my mum brings food.

We get home, and it's just like it always is. Our dog is there, and there's that funny smell in the corridor.

'The trouble is,' says Liv, 'she hasn't pooed yet.'

We check all our books. None of the manuals mention pooing.

Liv becomes distraught. 'Poor little baby,' she says, bursting into tears. 'She's not pooed in two days.' She sobs and sobs and sobs. I think: Oh my God ... I've known her be a bit mad before, but now she's going insane. And I know why. She's not slept in two weeks. I realize there's only one thing that matters: we've got to get her to sleep.

She fights it and fights it, but at 11 p.m. she feeds Grace again, and then somehow I persuade her: she must sleep. I promise I'll wake her up. I'm lying. There's no chance on earth I'm waking that woman if she falls asleep.

I take Grace away to a different room, and I arrange a bed on the floor. She cries, so I put my finger in her mouth, and she sucks at it. I like the feeling. So does she. We have a long, contented sleep. Every now and again we wake. We look at each other like young lovers. I put my finger back in her mouth. She sucks. Happy, we fall back to sleep.

In the morning, Liv appears. Grace and I are sleeping like newborn babies. My finger is bright red. I feel delighted that I've looked after a baby for the night. Liv sees the evil of what's happened. Grace still hasn't pooed. And now we've starved her for an entire night. And how do we know my finger is clean? We really need some help. We need my mother.

We call Val. She lives in Shrewsbury, which is three hours away. She promises to arrive immediately. She gets into her Saab and floors it. She arrives about ninety minutes later. She's a short smiling lady carrying an assortment of plastic bags. They contain food, babygros and, freakishly, some maternity bras that Val saved from her last campaign. SuperVal to the rescue. She tells us not to worry about the pooing. She reassures us there'll be plenty of poo later.

It's always the way!!!

Val arrives

Rule 12: Look at the world as if you're seeing it for the first time

January 2002, Stoke Newington

Now we face a stream of visitors. Half of these are relatives, whose mission is to claim the child for their family.

'She looks just like Hattie,' says my mum.

'Oh yes,' says an aunt, who's bearing a picture of Babar, 'she looks just like Uncle Peter.' I feel a hearty desire to smash Babar over her head.

'She's got your nose!' say my relatives.

'She's got Livy's eyes,' say Liv's, as if Grace were some kind of Mr Potato Head, who's using a combination of other people's features.

The other visitors are weird friends whom we've not seen in ages. I don't think: How sweet. Maybe we're going to be friends again soon! I think: Why am I making these people tea when I could be sleeping?

The best thing is being with Grace. I like it when she's hungry. She turns her head to her shoulder, and opens her mouth. She looks like she's calling for a cab. Except she does it with one eye shut, so she's making a pirate face. She looks like a pirate calling for a frigate.

I like it when she wakes up and cries; it gives me an excuse to see her. I change her nappies. I always lift both feet because someone told me that, if you lift just one foot, then you can dislocate the hips. I learn about winding . . . When a baby has had her milk, she must burp, or else the wind gets trapped inside and goes bad – like bad thoughts. This is called gripe. So I learn I must hold her upright. I discover I can squeeze gently on her lower back, and thus I can expel the wind. This is immensely satisfying. It's like playing the bagpipes except, instead of playing 'Scotland the Brave', you make burps. This is actually a better sound than bag-pipes. I'd love to see them redo the Edinburgh Tattoo one year. I'd dearly love to see a squadron of babies, all belching in unison.

At one point Grace is with Livy, screaming, and I say: 'Maybe she senses you're tense,' and I take her, and I bounce my knees softly, and she stops crying. In that moment, I see that Livy is a worrier, making life difficult for everyone. I realize I'm a world expert on childcare. Now I feel much happier about the whole thing. I take Grace downstairs, where we bounce slowly, and listen to Albinoni's cello con-certo. I sob gently. She stares at the lights on the ceiling. We go out into the garden, and enjoy the coolness of the night air. She looks around with a look of incredible wonder, and I feel that, if I can learn to copy that look, I will learn the secret of happiness. And we just stand there, and I have an alarming feeling that no one warned me about. I feel more love than I've ever felt before.

Two weeks later, a nurse comes round because Grace is two weeks old. This in itself is weird, since the nurse looks like Elvis Presley, although she talks in an East London accent. Cockney Elvis tells me that Grace has actually lost weight since birth. She recommends formula feed, which is the baby equivalent of the fried banana sandwich.

Livy says: 'But I've read breast is best.'

Elvis says: 'Yes, but formula has more calories. And it'll give Daddy something to do.'

'OK,' says Liv. 'Fine.' Elvis goes. Livy weeps. 'Oh God,' she says, 'I'm a bad mother . . . my milk doesn't work!'

So now I must do a formula feed at 1 a.m., so I must stay up watching telly. And then I find Grace snuffling to wakefulness, and then I change her and we both lie back, me on pillows, she on my raised knees. She sucks away on the bottle for fifteen minutes, and meanwhile we stare into each other's eyes, and I wonder what she's thinking about. I live in the city. No one looks at me all day, and I don't look at them. There's too much risk we might express love for each other. But Grace is only a baby; she doesn't know the rules. People complain a lot about babies at night-time, but sometimes they're better than Prozac.

Rule 13: Follow That Woman
(to hospital if necessary)

February 2002, Stoke Newington

The most notorious parenting book is *The Contented Little Baby Book* by Gina Ford, which all dads love since it's powerfully logical, and slightly fascist. I'll summarize it for you:

1. After the first month, you should force your child into a strict schedule of feeding and sleeping. It will make them contented, because they become well rested and well fed.
2. You should wake them so you can do the first feed by 7 a.m. This discourages them from sleeping all day, and waking all night.
3. You should feed your baby roughly every three hours. Don't let them snack. If they do, they will not drain the breast fully.
4. If they cry in their cots, check they haven't got dirty nappies, or wind. Then leave them. Babies must learn to settle themselves.

That is the theory, and it's a marvellous one. In practice this happens:

1. Baby doesn't want to eat every three hours. Baby takes the view that, if God didn't want her to suck on those things, He wouldn't have put them at mouth height and filled them with delicious

creamy milk. When Baby is not sucking on the breast, Baby cries. So does Mum. Mum feeds Baby.

2. Mum complains that her nips *really* hurt. Dad suggests she doesn't feed every fifteen minutes. Mum gives him a bad look.

3. Mum and Dad are still managing to get Baby to sleep at the right time, in the right place. But then Baby gets a cold. (Babies are contractually obliged to have 136 colds a year. They have a schedule they must stick to.)

4. Mum gets a cold as well. Mum is sick, tired and hopelessly emotional – a fatal combination. One night, Mum feeds Baby, and tells Dad to put Baby to bed.

5. Dad does. Baby screams. Dad thinks: I must let Baby settle herself.

6. Mum thinks: Baby is crying! Why the bloody hell is Dad doing nothing?

7. Dad goes outside. He pretends he's emptying the bin. Actually, he's having a fag. Baby is crying.

8. Dad brushes his teeth. Baby is still crying. Mum calls for Dad.

9. Dad arrives. Mum says: 'Did you check her nappy?'

   Already Dad feels on the back foot.

   He says: 'Yes. I did.'

   'Are you sure she hasn't got wind?'

   He says: 'Yes. I winded her.'

   Baby screams. Mum runs into Baby's room. It stinks of shit. Mum picks up Baby. Baby lets out a burp that shakes the very foundations of the house.

10. Mum gives Dad a look. It says: 'I don't know if I'm ever going to trust you again. You lied about our child.'

11. Mum changes Baby's nappy. Dad scuttles around fetching baby wipes, saying: 'She must have just done that, otherwise I would have smelled it.' Mum says: 'Not if you've been smoking.'

12. Baby cries more. They now look at Baby. Baby's got a runny nose, and swollen eyes. Baby's also got a touch of jaundice, and has gone yellow. Baby does not look well. Baby looks like a yellow goblin. A screaming, gleaming yellow goblin.

13. Dad says: 'Don't you think you'd better put her down? Gina Ford says —'

    'That woman,' says Mum, 'had no children of her own.'

14. Dad goes. Dad has not felt this bad since the Christmas when he deliberately burned his brother's present.

15. He pops out for another fag. Even outside the house he can still hear Baby crying. The whole street can. Baby's crying scratches the inside of Dad's head. Suddenly the crying stops.

16. Dad comes back in. Goes to bedroom. Mum is in bed with Baby. Breastfeeding. Mum gives him a wounded, triumphant look that says: 'Yes, I am feeding Baby. Don't try to stop me.' Mum looks satisfied, but guilty, all at once — a bit like a lioness that's just killed another antelope.

17. Dad can't leave it. He says: 'Gina Ford says . . . Erm.'

    Suddenly Mum bursts into tears. 'Why is Gina

Ford trying to keep me from my baby? I can't bear it!'

Real tears run down Mum's cheeks. They plop onto the sniffling yellow head of the child.

18. Mum says: 'Do you think we should take her to the hospital?'

Dad, terrified, says: 'No.'

Mum says: 'I'll just call them and see what they say.'

19. Mum rings the hospital. She asks the nurse if it sounds like her child has got pneumonia. Nurse asks her to describe the symptoms. Dad makes a half-hearted attempt to get hold of the phone. Mum gives him a warning look – a bit like the one that Rottweilers give before they take out the postman.

20. The nurse suggests to Mum she could visit the hospital.

Dad says: 'Nurse would say that. She doesn't want to get sued for negligence. I just think there are no situations which can't be solved by everyone having a damn good night's sleep.'

Mum says: 'Are you contradicting medical advice? Are you going to drive me to the hospital, or do you want me to take the bus?'

21. Dad drives Mum and Baby to hospital.

22. They wait in A and E. They start to realize they are the only middle-class people there. They see a youth with a knife wound. There's a drunken woman who's got one of her ears in the pocket of her jeans. Baby sleeps soundly.

23. After two hours, they visit Doctor. He says Baby has got a cold, some gripe and a spot of jaundice.

He says the best thing would be to have a good night's sleep. He says they were quite right to bring the baby in.

24. On the way home, Dad feels he was in the right about the whole incident. He's hoping Mum might say: 'I'm so sorry to have worried. It was very silly of me.' Dad is hoping that tonight Mum will kiss him as if she were Florence Nightingale, and he were a hardy little soldier who's fought some difficult battles today.

    She says: 'Are you OK?'

    He says: 'Yep . . . Bit tired . . . I just . . . I wish we'd stayed home.'

    She says: 'Don't you make me feel guilty. I didn't make you feel guilty when you put her to bed without even checking the nappy.'

    Dad doesn't argue any further. He concentrates on acting wounded.

25. Back home, Mum bursts into tears. Baby bursts into tears. They comfort each other with a marathon orgy of breastfeeding.

26. At a party, Mum mentions that Dad thinks Gina Ford is right. Three women turn on him with narrowed eyes. They wouldn't hate him more if he'd just confessed to torture. Simultaneously, they all say: '*That Woman* had NO children of her own.'

27. Three years later, the child is still not sleeping through till morning. Mum is going in, several times a night, to pat her head, or check the blankets haven't fallen off. Dad takes the view that the blankets probably haven't fallen off, and has started wearing earplugs. He's found that the

best ones are the coloured foamy ones from Quies. Each night, he squeezes them, puts them in, and they *gradually* muffle out the entire world and now he won't be getting up even if there's a bomb scare. Mum forgives him, but she expects him to do a hell of a lot of laundry.

Rule 14: Don't expect kids to bring you together

May 2002, Stoke Newington.
Grace is five months old

People say that having a baby teaches a man his purpose in life. That purpose is to provide (1) sperm, (2) cash and (3) free childcare. I've done the first thing, I can't do the second, so I must do the third. Grace is five months old, and Liv goes back to work.

She doesn't want to, but she's the only one with a guaranteed income. She's got a new City job, doing Ethical Investment for a big pension company. As I understand it, this is Liv's job ... She visits the CEO of a massive drug company. The CEO says: 'About the ten million you usually invest this time every year?' And Liv says: 'About the free drugs for African AIDS victims?' And then the CEO says: 'Ah, there's legal problems with supplying those.' So then Liv makes some phone calls and before you know it the *Financial Times* is carrying a front-page story saying: 'Investors warn drugs industry of backlash over AIDS crisis'. The piece carries a crafty quotation from Livy: 'It would be ironic if a sector dedicated to saving lives would come to have the pariah status of the tobacco industry.' I love the gentle sarcasm of that 'ironic'. Shortly after that, the drugs company calls Liv up, and says: 'We've straightened it out with the lawyers. We're going to give out the free AIDS drugs. Now . . . about the ten million?'

This seems a perfect job for Livy. She has to be sneaky in order to force people to do good. Which is sort of what she's doing with me. The trouble is Liv's boss has got children herself, but she works till past nine o'clock most nights. The boss has got staff. Liv has got me.

My mum comes when she can. I'd like her to come more often, but she's got her own life, and also we pay her, and Liv says: 'If you want her to come more often, you'll have to earn more money.' I don't have the BBC job any more, and I'm poor. So now I'm doing childcare, and I've got no money, and I can't get more money, because I'm doing childcare. The first time I walk to the park wearing a papoose I pass the big Irish family on the corner, which is Stoke Newington's homage to *Angela's Ashes*. I pass a malnourished teenage boy, who senses my discomfort. With a beautiful accent, he says: 'Jesus Christ! You look like a fucking eejit!' and I agree with every cell in my body.

It would be OK if I'd slept, but I'm up till 2 a.m., and I'm woken at 8 a.m., and I immediately go downstairs to find Liv. She says: 'You will remember to pick up my dry cleaning, won't you?' Then she leaves for work. While at work she calls me up every time she's in the toilet. She spends half her working day in the toilet. She goes in there to milk herself. It's the mum's equivalent of masturbation, but it produces more fluid.

On the phone, she complains she doesn't want to be at

work. She wants to be home with her new baby. I complain that I'm with the baby. I want to be out working. Liv has a romantic view of childcare. She thinks it's all about having picnics in a field strewn with daisies. She's wrong, I tell her. Childcare is one per cent inspiration; it's ninety-nine per cent walking around the house hanging socks on radiators.

I don't visit meadows strewn with daisies. I visit Baby Music, the cemetery and shops. I hang shopping on the handles of the buggy, right next to the dog lead, and the dog pulls because she's mad keen to choke herself to death on some chicken bones that some dick has just chucked out of their car window, and the buggy falls over, and the eggs smash, and Grace cries, and I'd be better at comforting her if I didn't feel like such a failure. This is not fun. At this point the Prozac of childcare has well and truly worn off. The tragedy of drugs is they work for a short time only. Same with childcare. I could probably take it if it was just once, but it's every day, and I'm not even good at it. I'm hopeless. I have the domestic instincts of the average smack addict. I feel tired and unbalanced. The sleepless nights have left me with a red-hot seam of anger inside.

I try to talk to Gary, who's my best friend. He hasn't a clue what I'm talking about. He's gay. His only commitment is going to the gym. He says to me: 'Ah, you're looking after your daughter! That must be so fulfilling. I bet you're great at that!' I want to say: 'I'm a man. If I'm great at something, I expect an award. I expect cash. I don't expect to be changing nappies at two in the morning, working with sewage, for no money, for someone who shouts at me.' But I don't. Gary produces my Radio 4 show and I don't want him to think I'm a loser he shouldn't work with. I learn to repress.

Liv comes home from work at seven. She wants a break from saving the AIDS victims of Africa. I want her to award me an MBE for my feat of doing a day's childcare. Baby food is splattered up the wall. The living room is a car crash of plastic objects, and dirty nappies, and damp socks.

She says: 'Did you fetch my dry cleaning?'

I say: 'No. I forgot. Sorry.'

I hand Grace to her, and go upstairs to try to write. Me and Liv have become a tag team. It's one in, one out.

that must be sooo fulfilling!

Rule 15: Find the Dad Manual

June 2002, Stoke Newington.
Grace is six months old

One day, I'm changing Grace, and I notice some used wet wipes have fallen down the back of the chest of drawers. I pull out the chest. I cause a cascade of nappies and creams and babygros. It suddenly occurs to me: 'My dad *never* did this!' I remember a postcard I used to have, which my dad sent me when I was three months old. He had gone to a kibbutz, because he wanted to find himself. This was 1970. I always used to picture him looking muscular and picking oranges. Now I'm picturing Val, on her own, with two kids. Suddenly I realize that, in the back of my head, is the Dad Manual. It's a record of everything that my dad did, as a parent. I know I'm programmed to repeat it. I want to be as spectacularly lazy as my dad was, but then that'll turn me into him. Worse, I don't even have the right to be lazy. At least my dad earned the cash. I see the truth of what Oscar Wilde said: 'Children begin by loving their parents. After a time they judge them. Rarely, if ever, do they forgive them.' I want to shout at Oscar Wilde too. He had two kids himself. He wrote them several sweet stories. You can bet he didn't have to fetch dirty wet wipes from behind the chest of drawers.

I get a brilliant idea for a TV show. It's called *The Superdad Championships*. Three dads are being filmed, *Big Brother* style, but they don't know it. Each dad has to load a broken buggy into the boot of the car when it's raining and a child is screaming, and a wife is telling him to put it the other way round. We compare technique as each dad chuffa-trains the spoon towards the baby's mouth. The dad gets points for calmness, efficiency, humour. He loses points when he starts shouting.

Livy arrives home. She looks at the mess. I want her to ask how many spoonfuls of carrot I managed to feed to our child.

She says: 'Did you manage to go to the dry cleaner's?'

I say, 'No.'

I pass Grace over.

I go upstairs, and I write out *The Superdad Championships*. I send it to Gary, who also makes TV shows. He ignores the proposal. It's appropriate. That's the tragedy about being a parent. If you do it well, no one notices. Except the kids, of course. But it'll take thirty years before they say anything, and, whatever you do, you know it won't be the good stuff they mention.

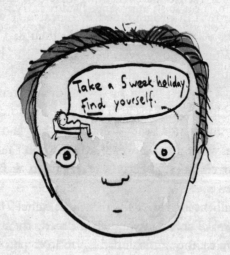

Rule 16: Give her an inch, she'll chuck you; give her six inches, she'll breed

July 2002, Stoke Newington. Grace is six months old. Liv's twenty-nine. I'm thirty-two

Sunday, 7.32 p.m. Grace is in bed. I'm lounging on the sofa reading books about parenting. They all have much the same advice, which they drag out for hundreds of pages with examples and box inserts. This is it:

1. Love them, but ignore tantrums.
2. Don't let them watch TV. Three hours a week, at the most. Otherwise you will sap their creativity.
3. Always use positive language. You don't say: 'Shut up. You're so annoying. Daddy is trying to shop.' You say: 'Be calm. Good girl. Now look out, and see if you can find the ketchup.'
4. Give them plenty of sleep, exercise and fresh vegetables.
5. Use the Naughty Stair.

OK, the books don't tell you what to say if your child says, 'Why is the stair naughty?' And they don't tell you *how* to love your children when you're worrying about money, and you can't work, and you're incapable of love. You could boil all the books down to one sentence: Feed them vegetables; make them exercise; don't show them porn. It's excellent advice, though. Very wise. I plan to pass it all on to my children. Meanwhile, I'm taking none of it myself.

I sling the books aside. The microwave pings. I go over and fetch my curry. Then I slump on the sofa with the *Sunday Times* Culture section that I took out of someone's bin. I can't leave the TV alone. The TV is like a dirty ex-girlfriend that I can't grow out of. Yes, I know that no good is going to come of the relationship. It leads to feelings of disappointment and envy. But sometimes, late at night, I find I'm still hanging around, hoping for some light relief.

I take out a felt tip and begin work on this evening's schedule. I'm thinking: *Seinfeld*, as is traditional as the 8 p.m. starter; then there's a Viewing Hole for half an hour, during which time I'll cut between *Will and Grace* and the documentary about the woman who lost her skin; the main course will be a *Fawlty Towers* double bill; *Peep Show* for dessert course. Then anything on Channel 5, as a kind of porn course. Then I'll lose Liv by saying, 'I'll clear up,' and I'll do *Match of the Day 2*, but then I'll cut, randomly, to *The Last Days of Kurt Cobain*. Handled correctly, I'll watch Kurt die, interspersed with shots of Michael Owen chipping the keeper. Who can imagine a more perfect end to the evening? After that I'll be so hyped up, I'll need some David Attenborough, because he calms me like Rohypnol.

Liv arrives. She says: 'Aren't you coming to bed?'

'Erm . . .'

'If you don't go to bed early, you'll be bad tempered in the morning.'

'But it's only eight o'clock.'

'Well, I was thinking . . . we could . . . sleep together? We could have sex.'

'Oh. You strumpet.'

In the privacy of my own head, I've just said the sentence: 'Do we *have* to have sex?' I feel like I've just been set extra homework. My libido has been locked away in a little

Tupperware box that's also filled with sterilizing pills. I'm a little flattered that she's asked though.

'Well . . .' she says, 'I thought we wanted another baby.'

Yes. We do. Sometime in the future. But *Seinfeld* is on *now*. And, anyway, you don't want to make love to me; you just want to conceive. I feel rejected.

'Well . . . what do you think?'

'About us having another baby?'

'Yes.'

I'm thinking: OK, I'll forgo David Attenborough, but you can't seriously expect me to miss *Match of the Day 2*!

I say: 'Isn't it a bit disloyal to Grace?'

'You're allowed to have more than one child.'

'Yes . . . though it causes global overpopulation.'

'If you have two, that's just replacing you. The national average is one point seven. We won't cause global over-population.'

'Though we might cause global warming.'

'Listen . . . It's not going to send the Maldives underwater if we have another baby.'

'It'll mean we won't go there ourselves.'

'But maybe we won't want to. I think Grace would love to have a baby.'

'She would. But she'll be furious when, months later, that baby is still there. Shouting at night.'

'That's only at first. Then it starts getting better.'

This is one of her favourite themes: the time when It Starts Getting Better. Some people say you've got to get them sleeping through the night. Some say you've got to get them to school. Parents with teenagers love to say: 'You wait. It gets worse.'

'Anyway,' says Liv, 'we wouldn't be doing it for her sake. We'd be doing it for ours.'

I look into her eyes. She looks into mine. It's the first time we've really looked at each other for a while.

'And we'd be doing it for her sake,' says Liv. 'The baby, I mean.'

'Assuming she's a girl,' I say.

'Which she probably would be.'

'Why?'

She seems to be suggesting I'm so unmanly I could never produce a boy. She's suggesting I have effeminate sperm. She's suggesting that, inside my balls, it's one big princess party.

'Because,' she says, 'we've had one girl already. There's medical research about this. Women all have a tendency towards one of the sexes. It's to do with the acidity in the vagina.'

'Hang on . . . you're saying you've got an acid fanny and it produces girls?'

'Sort of.'

'Well, now you put it like that, I can't wait to get to bed so I can see this acid fanny for myself. I don't think I've ever felt so aroused in my life. But why don't you watch *Seinfeld* with me first?'

She sits down next to me. Luckily Kramer skids in, and we both laugh. This is good. I need to buy myself a bit of time. I'm not against a new baby. I've met two sets of parents who've had just one baby. One is a very loving couple, who could only manage one child, and they treat her brilliantly. The other are prim control freaks who like clean houses, and fitted carpets, and never being in debt. The control freaks have just sold their house so they can move to an expensive area with good schools. This is the most pathetic, fearful action I've ever heard of. I want to be a big-hearted, free-spirited person with lots of noise and lots of fun and people running from room to room. I want another baby. But I feel a little hurt at the absolute plainness of the seduction. I'm a man; I want to be wooed.

We watch *Seinfeld*, and then we reach the Viewing Hole. I want to keep watching. I want to push onwards like a marathon runner. It's a tough schedule, but I know I can do it. I sigh. I switch off the TV, and go upstairs.

Our bedroom's not the velvet love palace it might be. On her side there are catalogues, cereal bowls and three different kinds of Calpol. On mine there are earplugs. Livy is sitting up in bed, penning a report called 'Socially Responsible Investment: The Quiet Revolution'. I'm delighted about Livy's Quiet Revolution. I just don't want it in my bed. And Liv's looked better, in all honesty, than she's looking now: a stone heavier, smelling of milk and baby sick, and looking like she could cry at any moment. I know I'm not at a physical peak myself. I've got a stomach that I never had before. I couldn't call it a beer gut. More a wine and curry gut. The other night she touched it, and I had to push her away.

I tidy up the whole place. I remove Calpol. I remove tissues. I remove loads of those packets of wet wipes with the aloe vera moisturizer that just smells like shit. Then I open the window. Then I go upstairs and fetch down my copy of *The Lord of the Rings*. Normally I read it at 1 a.m., after I've done Grace, because I can't sleep till I've found out what's happened to the hobbits.

I get into bed. I read Tolkien; she reads the Loftmasters catalogue. She says: 'Can we turn the light out?' I hate it when she says that. As if I haven't reached the age where I'm allowed to turn my own light out. As if I didn't know that, before you go to sleep, you must turn your light out. One day, I might visit prostitutes just so I can read a bit about the hobbits before I go to sleep. That'll teach her.

I keep reading. I read till nine o'clock. Aragorn is preparing for battle. Aragorn can fight giant monsters, but could he change a nappy? I turn the light out. I feel calm from the reading, but my imagination is buzzing. I notice that, unusually, there's someone lying in the bed next to me. She leans over and kisses me. I don't want her to kiss me. She's making my lips feel wet. And she's blocking my good nostril and I can't breathe. But she keeps on kissing me, and I catch her smell, which is like jasmine on a rainy June evening, and suddenly my body starts filling with hormones and I start to feel different. 'Hmmm ...' says a little voice in my mind. 'This is *nice* ...'

My head fills with my favourite fantasy ... It's 1900 Vienna. I'm Gustav Klimt. I'm thirty-eight, with a bushy moustache. I'm pressing young, luscious Anna Mahler against a wall. She looks like Livy. 'There is only one thing for it,' I say, 'complete physical union.'

There is only one thing for it: complete <u>Physical</u> Union.

Rule 17: Let babies play on the stairs

November 2002, Stoke Newington

Grace is ten months old and can sit up. She topples sideways like a drunk falling off a bar stool, but she can sit up. She doesn't crawl. She bum-shuffles, like a dog with worms. She can go upstairs, but she can't go down again. Babies are like teenagers at parties: they gravitate to the top. I've been tempted to stop her climbing, but then I see what a proud grin she has on her face as she climbs, so I haven't got the heart to stop her.

She's also got a gigantic head, which is flat on the top, like a helicopter pad. We call her Pad, for a joke. She said her first word. It was Dada. OK, she puked immediately afterwards – a mixture of pear and mashed carrot – but I still found that endearing.

She's doing great. But everyone else is suffering. The dog is looking permanently worried. As well she might. Liv is pregnant again, although she's hiding it from work. She's developed an incredible sense of smell, and has suggested that the dog might go and live elsewhere. I'm outraged by this. Dogs are unreconstructed sexists, who make the mistake of assuming the man is in charge. Accordingly, they give men more affection than they give women. When I scratch the dog's neck, she turns her head obligingly. When I scratch Livy's neck, she says: 'Can you go to IKEA? I've asked you three times already.'

The dog starts laying turds halfway up the stairs. She's sending a message to us. It's: 'Listen. Let's split. Why don't you have upstairs? I'll have downstairs. To make it easier, I've marked the edge of my territory.' I understand. The dog is protesting against the new regime in the house, a bit like the dad who thinks he can still have a Saturday morning lie-in. But Liv doesn't appreciate the subtle nuances of the dog's actions. She tells me angrily to tidy up the turds, as if I'd done them myself. She smacks the dog. She sends me to IKEA to buy those annoying plastic things that stop babies opening cupboard doors. She also tells me to stock up on Calpol. We always need more Calpol.

I'm still doing a hell of a lot of childcare. I've noticed that, if I try to work, Grace gets angry, and I get nothing done anyway, and the whole place gets even messier. So I don't work. I don't exercise. I see no one except a baby, a dog and some domestic appliances. In the kitchen, the sterilizer has made a depressing damp smell, a bit like warm swimming pool. I hate the sterilizer. I hate all the appliances, because they're all useless, or misguided. The smoke alarm is just there to tell you your toast is ready. The washing machine is there to dye everything a mucky grey colour. The dish-washer is just unhelpful. Its attitude is: 'I will wash the dishes, but only if you wash absolutely everything first.' I hate the Hoover. It's got a little knob on it, which offers you Maximum or Minimum suckage. (Minimum suckage: for people who are hoovering, for the sheer joy of hoovering. For people who just want to massage the dust.) There's only one appliance I like, which I took from my mum's house in a burst of nostalgia: the SodaStream. The SodaStream sits at the back of the cupboard, unwanted. It seems to be saying: 'I can still do it. I'm an entertainer. You have a party – I'll make Coca-Cola. Well … it looks like Coca-Cola. It tastes like shit.' I sense I'm becoming unusual. I'm imagining how appliances would talk.

One day my mum visits and I try to get writing. After an hour, I hit a problem. I think I'll make coffee. I'll ponder what I should do. I'll settle my head. I reach the kitchen. My mum says: 'Oh-don't-worry-I'm-about-to-do-the-washing-up-RIGHT-now-Grace-has-eaten-THREE-bowls-of-yoghurt-but-I-think-that's-FINE-don't-you-think-EXCUSE-ME-I'm-not-saying-that's-all-she's-eaten-NOW-have-you-written-to-Nana-even-if-you-just-send-her-a-card-that-would-be-fine-I-NEVER-know-where-you-leave-the-sterilizing-tablets-did-you-NOT-THINK-of-KNOCKING-THROUGH-the-wall-to-connect-the-kitchen-to-the-living-room-I-really-DON'T-KNOW-why-you-moved-from-Kentish-Town.'

It's classic Mum talk. It's a bizarre mixture of apology, recrimination and maverick property advice. My mother presents a chaotic world where walls can be knocked through, where the past hasn't happened, where nothing makes sense, but on the good side she's managed to do two loads of washing. Strangely, this doesn't settle my head. So I decide to hide from her, and I get some work done.

She stays two days, and then she goes.

That evening, Liv comes home from a conference in Amsterdam. I want her to tell me about it. She wants to switch off from thinking about work. She says: 'How are you?'

I say: 'Well, I'm not getting any writing done, and it's driving me mad.'

'Yes, you are!'

'I'm not. If I'm looking after Grace, I'm still tidying up at ten at night.'

And she says: 'Do you want to pay for more childcare? You don't have any money. I'm the only one with a regular wage. That's why I've supported us both for the last few years.'

'No, you haven't. I've had money as well.'

'Not as much and we can't count on it.'

'But I need to write.'

'I've been working flat out to pay for us both.'

'I don't want you to be.'

'Nor do I. I want to be at home looking after Grace. The least you can do is try to be grateful. I'm giving you a gift. Why don't you enjoy it?'

I'm a man. The only gift I want is free time, so I can do some work to recover my self-esteem. I realize she's become the husband and I've become the naughty wife. Husband's saying: 'I've paid for all this, you lucky girl. So you better enjoy it.'

I try explaining this to Livy, and she says: 'Listen, if you're not making any money doing your comedy and your writing, maybe you should get another job. Do something else.'

And I say: 'Yeah, like what?'

'I don't know,' she says. 'Find out what you're good at, and make money from it.'

'That's like ... an existential crisis, speeded up. You're saying: find out who you are, brand it, make money. Quick. How am I supposed to do that?'

I fall silent. I'm trying to be upbeat about it, but the truth is she's got me. I'm thinking: God, what the hell else am I going to do with my life? I must be very talentless to get to this position. I'm in my thirties and I've got no job. I'm developing post-natal depression.

And then I recognize what's happening. And I shout: 'Hang on a second – what are you saying? I've already got two jobs. I do comedy, and I write. Sometimes I even act.'

The problem is I haven't any time to work, because I'm looking after a child.'

And she says: 'Look. I've been at work all day. Will you stop shouting at me?'

'I'm not shouting at you. Don't say I'm shouting.'

'You're shouting now. Listen. I've really got a headache.'

'Fine,' I say, 'I'll go and sleep on the mattress upstairs.'

And I go upstairs, and I sleep on the mattress.

As I lie there, I indulge my new fantasy ... One of Livy's girlfriends approaches me at a party. She says: 'Andrew, I want you to keep this secret, but I'd like to have your baby.' And of course I politely rebuff her, but I'm still deeply flattered that she sees me as a Sperm Lord, an outstanding provider of quality seed ... One afternoon, I'm out on my bicycle, and I decide I must call in to see her. I knock at the girlfriend's door and remove my cycle helmet. She answers. 'I just want your baby,' she says, staring into my eyes. 'We could use a syringe.' 'You lovely, silly, luscious woman,' I say. (I'm very caddish in this fantasy. I've got a pencil-thin moustache.) 'The syringe won't be necessary.'

I sleep a fevered, angry sleep. Suddenly the sun is on my face. We have no curtains in the upstairs room. I look at my watch. It's 10 a.m. A Saturday.

And then I hear a noise, a shuffling noise. It's the sound of babygro on carpet. It's the sound of a baby coming up the stairs to see me. I crawl from bed. I look over the banister, and see her making her way towards me like a chubby salamander. She's determined. I know I must wait.

I retreat into the bedroom, but I leave the door open. I say: 'I can heaaaaaarrrr you ... I can hear you *coming* ...' I can hear baby chuckles, which is the finest sound on this earth. Eventually a massive grinning head appears at the top of the stairs. It looks like the sun coming over the horizon,

71

but it's bigger. And sunnier. In her mind, she's just climbed the North Face of Everest. She thinks I am an angel whom she sees on the summit. I'm better than that. I'm Daddy. And I think: I'm proud to be a Stay-at-home Dad, but I can think of a better title. I shall think of myself as a Trophy Husband.

her massive head appears at the top of the stairs

Colonel Raff Raffington
(Head of Security)

Rule 18: Forgive those that harm you or you'll suffer for it

Spring 2003, Stoke Newington

We're getting the hang of having a child. You just have to give up on everything that's not either work, or childcare. And you have to get as much help as possible.

We've employed this guy called Mark, who's making a new garden fence. But he's separated from his ex, and they've got a kid, so he's always turning up four hours late with the kid. It's difficult to know where you stand on that. On the one hand, it's nice he's looking after his kid. On the other hand, we're paying him.

He knocks down the old fence, then he disappears.

So there's no fence now, which is of great interest to Raff. Now I've enlarged my pack, the dog respects me more. To her, I'm now The President. She sees herself as my Head of Security. She calculates that the removal of the fence might allow an invasion from our three biggest enemies: (1) squirrels, (2) foxes, (3) other border terriers.

Liv is outside now, inspecting the wreckage. Grace is at

her feet, arranging stones along the wall. It's a Friday. Officially, that means I'm writing, she's on childcare and she'll want to do something creative with Grace, like making cakes together. In practice, she thinks I'm pissing about doing nothing and, if she needs help, she'll ask for it. Being a dad is like being an unpaid GP. You're always supposed to be On Call. And you must have a perfect professional manner.

But I really need to go to the toilet. I immediately wonder what I'm going to read. I pick up a newspaper, which tells me about the terrorists who are living on the other side of Hackney. In the past, I've been an arch liberal about terrorists. Now I see the truth in what Al Murray says: 'When you become a parent, you become more right wing. Thank God Hitler never had kids!'

I go to the toilet. Before sitting, I delay a moment. I have no privacy any more. I never seem to manage the toilet without someone trying to come in. I decide to risk it. I feel rebellious, in fact. I'm going to do it. I open the doors and release the bombs.

I hear terrible screeching. I hear a shout:

'Andrew! Andrew! Quick!'

Oh no. Oh, leave me alone.

Liv continues screaming: 'Andrew! Quick! Raff has gone through Kim's flap!'

'What?!' She's making no sense. Who is Kim? And what's my dog doing in her flap? I picture the dog, wearing a lady as a hat.

'The *neighbour*!' Liv shouts. 'Raff's gone down the neighbour's cat flap. She's about to attack the cat.'

Oh my God. This is not good. Kim is our neighbour. Her boyfriend just left her. Last week, I was in the garden, and I heard her weeping in the bath. This is the noble, blameless woman whose cat we are about to kill. I'm trying to wipe up in a hurry. It's not easy. I feel like a gigantic brown felt-tip pen that will never dry up.

I run downstairs. I jump over the wall. I look through Kim's kitchen window.

The dog has cornered the cat between the oven and the fridge. She's barking like crazy, and is obviously psyching herself up for the final attack.

Liv says: 'Break the window, and stop it.'

I'm middle-class man in crisis. I don't want to break the window.

I stoop, and shout through the cat flap. 'Raff! Raff! Stop it!'

Liv says: 'Break the bloody window.'

Grace is watching me over the wall.

I smash the window. I break in like Jackie Chan.

The dog is encouraged to see The President arriving. She wants to impress. She leaps at the cat. She terminates with extreme prejudice. She grabs the cat's neck, and shakes violently. I don't know what that cat said to her, but it must've been bad.

I grab the dog. I say: 'Raff, BAD!' I smack her. I hurl her out the window.

I pick up the cat.

I can see the cat is dying.

I'm pretty damn sure it's almost dead.

What am I going to do?

The cat is dead. Am I going to bury her? Won't Kim want to bury her? Should I wrap her in plastic and put her in our freezer? What am I supposed to do?

The cat moves. I see she's alive. I see I must speed to the vet's. I imagine the vet holding a tiny little defib, just like they have on *ER*. The vet will shout: 'Clear!' The cat will miaow back to life.

I wrap the cat in a blanket, and I hurry to the vet's. As I go into the vet's, I'm not confident about this cat's health. I'm hoping she's just gone rather stiff. I go straight through to the back room. I put the cat down.

The vet says: 'Your cat is dead.'

I look at him. I say: 'Are you sure?'

The vet touches the cat. 'She's completely stiff . . .' I look at the cat. She's frozen with her mouth open. I touch her sandpaper tongue. I wonder what I'm supposed to do with her. For all I know, Kim might want to stuff her, and use her for sanding rough surfaces.

The vet says: 'Would you like us to keep her for you?'

I'm thinking it might put me in a good light if Kim knows the cat is at the vet's. I could even make out the cat died here. 'Yes.'

Trembling, I go. As I leave the vet's, I notice a cage of kittens in the corner. I wonder if I should take one home. See if the dog wants another go.

Next door there's a glass shop.

I go in. There's a cockney bloke. About twenty-six. Shaved head. Chewing gum. Spurs shirt. I ask him for a new kitchen window.

He asks for my address.

'Oh,' I say, 'it's not actually my address . . . It's my neigh-bour's.' I tell him the story. 'Perhaps I shouldn't fix the window. Is that an abuse of trust?'

He says: 'Mate, the moment you killed her pet: that was the abuse of trust right there. If I were you, I'd fix her bloody window.'

I tell him to come round. I go home. I clean up Kim's kitchen.

The bloke comes round, and he puts in new glass. I repair

the fence using string and an old plastic sandpit. Liv comes out and says: 'You have to call Kim.'

'Why do *I* have to call Kim?' I say.

'It was you who didn't break the window. How much more provocation did you need?'

'Yes, but ... you let the dog out. Until the fence is mended, the dog shouldn't be in the garden.'

Liv and I have been together for four years now, and we've learned the art of sustaining long-term relationships: you must blame everything on your partner. It's a constant tactical battle.

She says: 'I'm making tea for Grace.' She walks into the kitchen. Over her shoulder, she says: 'Please call Kim now.'

I flick through the Yellow Pages, and I find Kim's work number. I ask for her.

Unfortunately, she comes to the phone straight away.

I tell her what happened. Except I make out it happened in the garden. I'm admitting to the Cat Slaughter. I'm keeping quiet about the Forced Entry.

I say: 'Kim, is there anything I can do?'

She says: 'Well ... I've never had dinner with you and Livy.'

I say: 'God, you're always welcome. Even when ...' I trail off. What am I trying to say? Even when we haven't just killed your cat. 'Can you do tonight?'

Kim can.

She comes round at eight. We eat dinner. We drink wine. Liv goes to bed at eleven.

At midnight, I say: 'Erm ... shall I get out another bottle?' I do say 'erm', because that's middle-class code. It means: I'm making you an offer that you're not supposed to accept.

Kim says: 'I'd *love* another glass of wine.'

I'm thinking: I killed your cat. If you want to play naked Twister, I can't really say no.

Kim says: 'Do you know … I've always wanted to have children. And now I'm thirty-nine …' She trails off. For an awful moment, I think she's asking me to father her child. That seems too much to ask, even in the circumstances. She continues: 'And I've been wanting to move to the country-side, because I might have more luck finding a man. So now the cat has gone, it makes it easier. Everything happens for a reason.'

I say: 'Well, that's perhaps something good that's come out of this. But, Kim … I'm very sorry all the same.'

'I know,' she says. 'Thank you.'

I pour us both a glass of wine.

She says: 'She's an awfully nice girl, you know – Grace. And you look after her very kindly. I've noticed the way you talk to her.'

I'm stunned by her forgiveness. 'Kim!' I say. 'Thank you very much.' I realize I might choke up, so I hide it by giving her a hug. Kim pats me softly on the back.

After two days, I'm still cross with Raff, and she's still skulking.

Liv says: 'What's wrong with you two?'

I say: 'This is important. I'm disciplining her.'

She says: 'Do you think she understands that? Are you going to carry on forever? Wasn't it more pleasant when everyone was getting on?'

I look at Raff. She's skulking moodily in her basket. She's staring at a spider, wondering whether to kill it. I say: 'Raff, come here.' She does. I scratch her neck. She turns her head obligingly. Then she goes to the back door. She looks out, like a sentry, for more cats.

Rule 19: If you can't resolve a problem, find a distraction

April 2003, Derbyshire. Grace is fourteen months old

Friday, 8 p.m. We're driving to Derbyshire to spend the weekend with my cousin Hen. Livy is talking about how we're going to avoid sibling rivalry. She's also navigating. We're driving round a roundabout for the third time.

A text arrives from Hen. Liv reads it out: 'Where are you? I'm not feeling great, and don't know whether to stay up. But can't wait to see you. Hen X.' This encapsulates my cousin's personality: she offers professions of love; she's trying to control us; she wants us to know she's suffering on our behalf. Liv sighs. Since we're visiting my family, it'll be my fault if the weekend's not a success.

'Remind me,' she says. 'Why are we seeing Hen?'

Cos as an eight-year-old she'd lure me into cupboards, and we'd give each other Chinese Burns, or Butterfly Kisses, and all the things children do before they understand that they're basically being horny, and preparing to commit unspeakable deeds with their own cousin. Also we're seeing her because she's one of the most intelligent adults I know. She reads books, and not just ones about baby elephants who are looking for their mummy. She plays the harpsichord, and is an expert on early Bach. We play music too, but most of it concerns a sailor whose tragedy was that 'All that he could see see see/Was the bottom of the deep blue sea sea sea'.

'Cos she's got two kids of the right age,' I say. She has: William (5) and Maud (2). 'And maybe we'll learn something about sibling rivalry. Plus, she's got a really nice pad.'

This is true. Hen used to work in the City. Not for long. She didn't earn much, but she developed an overwhelming thirst for wealth. Her home has got stone steps, and mysterious doorways, and it's all furnished in Designer Peasant style. Her Aga-ed kitchen is migrating around the mansion, one room at a time. Hen is rich. She simply *adores* the Simple Life, and employs staff to help her do it. They follow her around the world flying Economy while she goes First Class.

So ... Two hours later. I'm with her, eating a feast. I've eaten half a roasted lamb. I'm drinking 1997 Sauternes. I've moved on to a caramelized lemon tart. It's probably the most delicious dinner I've ever eaten. Liv's in bed. A Polish lady is tidying. She's called Gosha. Hen is cutting herself some more onion tart, while discussing her husband, who's the twice-divorced finance director of a large petrol company. Strangely enough, I've never met him, but, to me, the words 'divorced', 'finance director' and 'petrol' never promised romance. They promised wealth. And there's nothing wrong with marrying someone because they're rich. There's nothing wrong with getting into a ring to wrestle a polar bear, but you'd have to anticipate certain consequences. I may be doing an injustice to the petroleum finance directors of the world. Perhaps they are a sensitive breed. Perhaps they return home every night bearing flowers, which they immediately sprinkle on their wives' bodies, while listening to the Bee Gees' greatest love songs.

'I love him,' she says. 'No, I *do* love him actually, but I don't think he loves me.'

Hen is trying to look poised and tragic like Marlene

Dietrich. The trouble is I'm distracted by her tits. That woman is addicted to boob jobs. She can never get the size quite right. Sometimes those tits go up and down more often than house prices.

'He *certainly* never tells me he loves me,' she continues.

'I never tell Liv I love her,' I say. 'I *do* feel love for her, but usually when I'm kissing her, or looking at her through a window. In fact, I only love her when there's no chance in hell I'll have to tell her.'

'No, but you do love her, so we're completely different.'

I'm thinking: We're different in that I believe my partner is the right person, and that helps make her right. You believe your divorce, handled correctly, will get you a big house and 100K a year.

'I just don't think he's my dream man,' she says.

Now I want to beat her like a gong. 'Love is a myth,' I say, 'used to sell books and underarm deodorant. It's a brief state of arousal brought on by beauty, strong chemicals or money. Don't use it as an excuse to break up your family.' And I dearly *want* to add: 'You can't love someone if you hate yourself. If you spend enough time with someone, they become a mirror of you. And if you look in a mirror, Hen, you're always going to see a walking hairstyle with weird fake tits.' And then I wonder why I'm getting so worked up about this subject.

'I'm tired,' she says.

'Yeah. Me too. But thanks for staying up and giving us dinner. It was delicious.'

I kiss my cousin, and go up to bed.

Liv is sleeping sweetly, so I have no problem feeling love for her. I whisper in her ear: 'Love is in the air, darling. But so is acid rain.'

Rule 20: Expect hatred;
praise affection

April 2003, Derbyshire.
Grace is fourteen months old

The next morning, everyone is playing in the big garden. It's got a pond. It's got apple trees. It's got a tennis instructor who arrived earlier, and there was a tantrum when the oldest child was forced out of a Spiderman outfit and into tennis whites. William had to make it clear to his mother exactly how much he resented that. 'Spiderman would never have a tennis racket,' he announced, with a persuasive logic. 'The racket gets in the way of his webs.'

According to his mother, Will has ADD, a Complexity of Food Issues and a powerful obsession with Spiderman. No one comes right out and says it, but everyone in the family hints that Will would be fine if his mother stopped Googling for medical conditions for him to suffer from. They reckon Hen's whole family isn't suffering from anything that couldn't be solved by a damn good recession that would stop them travelling to Aspen twice a month to visit their third home.

I ask Hen how she is.

'I'm fine. I'm blissful,' she says. 'I've just got a small migraine.'

This is no surprise. She is the sort of person who never has a headache. It's always a migraine. One time, she was sick. She was, she announced, 'having a gastral attack'. She feels she's got a monopoly on suffering. She also feels that she's rich, so someone must be attending to her troubles. I realize there's an unspoken contract about this weekend: Hen is giving me 1997 Sauternes; in return, I must play with her kids, in the absence of the much-loved, soon-to-be-divorced husband. I reckon one hour should do it. I suggest Hen lies down, and go off to play with her kids.

I make damn sure she appears at the very moment I'm cutely searching through the bushes with her children, looking for creatures. Maud finds a snail. She gives it to William.

'Oh, that is *sooo* sweet!' says Hen. 'William, do you love Maud?'

William says: 'No!' He quietly drops the snail to the floor, and crushes it underfoot. It makes a satisfying crunch. I look at William. I realize his mum is actually right about him. He's undeniably different. I like him. We just haven't wanted to accept the ADD thing since, in a family, no one wants to acknowledge anyone else has a problem. In families, everyone thinks sympathy is in short supply. They all want to hog it to themselves.

Hen says: 'William, you're just joking ... You love her. Do you love her?'

'Nooo!' says William. 'I HATE her.'

Hen puts on her Fierce Voice. 'William, you're actually being very rude, and rude boys can't go inside to watch *Bob the Builder*. Do you love Maud?'

'NOOO!!!' says William, refusing to lie, even for *Bob the Builder*. 'I hate her and I want to KILL her by stamping on her head.'

I think that's it. That's our lesson. This is how we're going to cope with sibling rivalry. We'll try to make games that include us all. We'll praise the smallest crumbs of sisterly affection. But we'll expect hatred.

Rule 21: Distrust the nesting instinct

April 2003, Stoke Newington

Liv is reaching her due date. She's now ninety per cent insane. She's obsessed with getting the baby out within the next few days. We've been invited on holiday in ten days' time. She woke at six this morning. She immediately fired up the computer, and started buying furniture. Then she set to work on the bathroom.

I wake as she empties a drawer of my hair products into the bin. I spring from bed. 'Darling ... I still use those!'

She picks up some Hair Fudge. 'You got this in 1999!'

'I use it sparingly.'

'Listen. Can you drive me to Colindale? I need to look at a wardrobe.'

'I've got a lot of work to do before the birth.'

'Why?'

'I've got to write my website. I've got to finish a sit-com. I've got gigs.'

'Those are all self-imposed deadlines. Why have you set them? You can work when she comes.'

'We both know that's a lie. For the next three months, my main activity will be standing in my pants, rocking a baby, while searching desperately for the Calpol.'

I go to the kitchen and start work. She follows me.

'Sorry, darling,' she says. 'It's just ... nesting instinct.'

'Love ... birds line their nests with sticks and feathers. They don't cram them with wardrobes. They don't throw out perfectly useful hair products. You seem to think that baby's first thought's going to be: I can't believe I've been born to such slobs. Right, I'm going back in!'

'I can't believe I'm spending the rest of my life with someone so moody.'

'So ... what? Just before giving birth you want us to split up?'

That was the wrong joke. She bursts into tears. I edge towards the door.

'You're inhuman!' she says. 'I'm crying and you won't even comfort me.' I comfort her. I even say I love her. I do love her, but definitely not when she cries. It makes me feel accused.

Two hours later, I'm driving her to Colindale. And she's good as her word. She doesn't buy that wardrobe. She just looks at it. Then we dine in the Colindale McDonald's – a place that Michael Winner has yet to review. She is craving a Vegeburger, although she's going to have it without the bun, and without the garnish.

We get home. I go to my office and start work. OK. First of all I arrange the transfers for my Fantasy League football team. She comes in.

'We need to get this baby out in the next three days,' she says. 'Let's have sex. The sperm could stimulate labour.'

I've heard better chat-up lines than this.

'Imagine that for the poor baby,' I say. 'She's all secure, in her tiny pink home. Suddenly a huge snake bursts through the floor. Repeatedly. Then it sprays slimy fluid everywhere. Next thing she knows, she's standing on her head, trying to squeeze through a tight tunnel.'

'Whatever!' she says. 'Just wank on your own. I'll scoop it inside!'

I know she's sort of joking. But, Lord, in my whole life, I've never imagined a love act as depraved as the one she's just described. I have to talk to her.

I say: 'Love. Listen. I'm feeling angry because –'

'I *knew* you were angry with me!'

'No no no! I'm not angry *with* you. I'm angry because I've also got things I need to do before the birth. I've got work.'

'I know!' she says. 'You're a nightmare!'

She bursts into tears again. They say that women forget the pain of childbirth or they'd never do it again. Similarly, men must forget the pain of living with a pregnant woman, or the whole world would be like China. Families would have one child each. They'd also have fewer wardrobes. Men would spend a lot of time wanking on their own. No one would ever scoop it inside, though. That shouldn't happen anywhere. That's the wrongest thing anyone has ever suggested. Only a pregnant woman could think of it.

they better be hoovering out there or I'm NOT coming out

Rule 22: Don't get high on your wife's supply

April 2003, Hackney

A week later. A Wednesday evening, 8 p.m. I've got a comedy gig tonight, but Livy is not officially due for three more days. She seems fine, though. A rare mood of calmness seems to have settled over her. We should be OK. We know everything about childcare now. We've found out we're having a girl. We've decided on the name Cassady. We've not consulted anyone.

I cycle off to the comedy club, dressed as a cub scout. I'm worried about the gig. I never used to worry about comedy; I did it for fun. Now whenever I go onstage I need it to go well. If it doesn't, it means I'm in the wrong job, which means I get tense onstage, which is not what audiences want. So I've turned to drugs. I now smoke a joint before working. It's for professional reasons. Audiences like me more when I'm slightly stoned. Tonight, though, I've used up my weed and, instead, I've eaten my magic mushrooms. I can feel them coming up as I cycle through Newington Green.

Liv calls. I get my phone out, but keep cycling. 'I think my waters have broken,' she says.

'OK,' I say, 'I'll come straight home.'

'Don't worry. I can't imagine anything's going to happen.'

I cycle on till I reach Great Ormond Street children's hospital. The symbolism is too much. I return home. I'm tripping slightly, but ready to take charge.

We drive to Homerton Hospital in Hackney. We ask to

go to the Water Birth section. This is an inspired request. It means we have a whole wing to ourselves, and it's very peaceful. The midwife comes over, and Liv is breathing away, and swirling her hips, and we're both caning it on the gas and air. It's going nicely with the mushrooms. We don't have music this time. I've got music in my head, and I'm concentrating on Liv's breathing. I'm holding her, she's gyrating, we're doing well. We don't even have the midwife for most of it. She sees that we're getting on fine, and she disappears out of the room.

Then at 11.50, the midwife comes in. She suggests Liv gets into the water-birth pool.

'Can I get in as well?' I ask. I've seen that in the photographs.

'There's no time for that,' she says.

Liv gets into the pool, and almost immediately, at 12.03 a.m., the baby shoots out of her. She's fired across the pool like a bar of soap squeezed from a fist. The midwife takes her out of the water, and Cassady starts screaming. She screams for half an hour solid. She's furious. We're all trying to give her the breast, but she's too angry to suck it. The crying sounds raw and painful. It sounds like a crow being struck with a stick. Immediately, we learn a crucial fact about Cassady. She's got a terrible temper; we'd do anything to avoid it.

At three in the morning, I'm driving through Hackney. I feel very calm, and very happy.

And then, the next day, I'm just thinking about Grace. How is she going to take this? She's fifteen months old now, and she can say thirty words. I counted them all up. There were some strange ones, like Yoghurt, and Avocado – 'Gogo', and 'Cado' – which proves we're definitely middle-class. We've told her all about the arriving baby. Also we've employed a Philippine lady – Elsa – who's going to stay with us for a few months to help out. Elsa's very glad. She's been living with her sister in Dagenham. She needs the money too. She's got children of her own back in the Philippines. She left them there when the youngest was only eighteen months old.

When I get back to the house, Grace and Elsa have gone out to the shops. I carry Cassady into the house in a baby car seat, and I put her on a coffee table.

Grace comes home. I want to stop her in the corridor, and give her a last speech that will prepare her for what's about to happen. But she comes straight into the living room and sees Cassady.

'Baby,' she says. 'MY baby!'

That baby is me, three hours old. That little boy is my brother Robert. He's just met me for the first time. He looks – rather presciently as it turned out – extremely worried.

Cassady

by Grace and Andrew Clover

One day I came home and there was a baby

"This is Cassady." said Mummy, she came out of my tummy."

"How?" I said

"She undid the tummy button and climbed out," said Dad.

"She's brought you a present." said Mum

It was a train set with 2 men. I did not see how Cassady made it in the tummy.

"why did she get me a present?" I said "she wanted you to be happy we've got a baby," said Mum.

I was happy we had a baby

I was not happy that, after a long time, that baby was still there.

at night she shouted and shouted and shouted

She mixed all the playdough together. She said she'd made a cake.

I thought she'd ruined the playdough

I did a picture of a smiley king on a horse and Mummy said that's lovely

she did a poo in the bath and I had to get out quick and tell Granny but she did not believe me

Cassady did a big scribble and she said it was a picture of me and Mummy said that's lovely but it was just a mess

I said to Mummy "I think we should send Cassady away in a big balloon."
Mum said: "I'm sending you both away to school. And you are in charge."
Next day we went to school together.

I was pleased because I like being in charge. At story time I put my hand on her back in the scary bit

at break time I sat next to Cassady, and not Leo Bingham who has green bogey worms, and also he steals biscuits.

in Sleeping Lions I went next to Cassady and not next to Orion Milligan who pulls hair and looks up skirts

and when we got home Mum was cross because Cassady had painted on the wall and I was sorry for Cassady but a bit glad because I had done some drawings but Mum did not notice.

At bath time Cassady got rude and did a funny dance

then she fell down the toilet and we laughed because she looked so funny but she didn't mind

"tomorrow," said Mummy, "I've got to take Cassady away in the car."

And I cried because Cassady is my sister and she is shouty and messy but I love her and don't want her to go away

"We'll be back at tea time," said Mum, "and then you can play Mummy and Baby".

And I was pleased because I like babies, and I like Cassady.

Rule 23: Parenting is a game of chess. Play to win

June 2003, Stoke Newington

All couples play a game called Parent Chess. The winning parent gets free time to themselves. Example:

> *Dad is lounging on sofa. He hears Mum's key in front door. He quickly starts washing up. This is Tactic One: never be caught out doing nothing.*

MUM: You OK?

DAD: Yep. Bit tired.

> *This is an exchange of pawns. Both parents have pleaded tiredness. They're indicating they may be physically incapable of more childcare. A good opening position.*

MUM: What are we doing tonight?

> *Mum has brought out a knight. Probing. Dad looks into his mental diary and sees nothing except 'find worming tablets' and 'try to do tax return'.*

DAD: Dunno. I'd like to see Gary.

> *His rook attacks.*

MUM: But I *never* see you! I thought we were having a quiet night in!

> *Mum is using the Standard Blocking Technique. She's saying: 'If I can't go out, you can't either.' She's prepared to lie, to make her case. Mum is the only adult Dad ever sees.*

DAD: I'll do stories. Then go out later. You go out tomorrow.

> *He's playing confidently. Bringing out a bishop.*

MUM: Darling ... Tomorrow it's my mum's birthday dinner. Have you forgotten?

His bishop is captured. Now he's in trouble.

DAD: What? I've got a gig tomorrow!

He's brought out his other knight. This is a strong move. Rules state that both parties can always go out for a professional engagement.

MUM: Is this an important gig? How much are you earning?

She advances her bishop. A vicious counterattack.

DAD (*weakly*): Forty quid. I want to practise some new material.

He blocks with his pawn. It's a terrible move.

MUM: I can't cancel my mum's birthday so you can earn forty quid. When did you accept it?

Her knight is putting him in check. She's suggesting the gig isn't important. She's hinting his professional life isn't important. She's moving in ruthlessly to achieve her objective: she wants them both to attend her mother's dinner. In fact, she wants more. She wants to go alone, while he babysits.

DAD: They called me this morning.

Dad has countered with another pawn. A hopeless move. They both know he should have checked the calendar.

MUM: Well ... Can't you call and cancel?

Mum is threatening Dad's queen. This is extraordinarily aggressive play.

DAD (*weakly*): OK.

He's surrendered his queen.

MUM: Why don't you do it now?

Mum takes queen.

DAD: By the way, Gary asked if I want to go to a festival this weekend. He's got a spare ticket.

Dad has advanced a pawn, and reintroduced the queen. But the queen can be immediately recaptured. This is a desperate move. She's never going to let him go to a festival. It will last all weekend.

He'll return bad-tempered, tired and incapable of decent childcare for days to come. He doesn't even know why he's mentioned it. But then . . .

MUM: Go! Sounds like fun.

This is unprecedented. She's let the queen go. What's going on?

DAD: Thanks . . . sure?

He's trying to move his queen out of trouble.

MUM: Sure.

She's stealthily advancing a rook.

DAD: I'll go and do stories, then.

He moves his knight.

MUM: By the way, I was thinking about Christmas. I don't want to spend it with your family. My mum's booked us a cottage. I said we'd spend Christmas with her. I've sent her a deposit.

Mum lunges forward and takes his king. She's gained Christmas – the ultimate prize. Mum is the champion. Mum is Garry Kasparov. Dad must try harder, or stop resisting.

Queen Mum

Pawn Dad

Mini Detective

Rule 24: If you want valuable things, value what you have

September 2003, the South of France

When Grace is born, our friend Kara gives her a small brown bear. Grace receives other bears, but she sees very quickly that they're just toys. She sees that the brown bear is special. I gave him a name, George Boujnim, The Famous Belgian Bear. If he's missing, Liv says: 'Have you seen that Belgian?' As soon as Grace can talk, she gives the bear her own name. She calls him Bear Bear.

May 2003, Grace loses him. This is a disaster. Cass is only two months old. I'm thinking: If we lose Bear Bear now, things are going to really kick off. Psychologists say that sibling rivalry is at its most intense when the older child is two. They say that sibling rivalry feels to a two-year-old what heartbreak feels like to a teenager.

Grace is nearly two. At night, she won't sleep. She shouts 'bear bear bear bear bear' and her face is filled with puffy outrage that things could ever get this bad. One Saturday, I try six shops, and I finally find Bear Bear at Hamleys. I buy three matching bears, and I find a smaller white bear, who I buy for Cass. We'll call it Bear Bear's Baby.

I get home. I put two of the bears in a drawer upstairs. Liv sees it. She says: 'Look. You've made a Bear Bear cloning factory.'

'Yes,' I say, 'but you must forget you ever saw this. This is top secret.' Then I go out to the garden where Grace is sitting on a towel, examining a bag of coloured pegs. I hide Bear Bear just out of sight, and I watch. I feel like a farmer who needs to bond a lamb with a different ewe. After a few moments, Grace turns. Her face smiles the biggest smile I've ever seen, and she comes straight over.

She loses him a couple of days later. Liv says it happened when they went walking to the cemetery, but I know Liv's seen my spare bears. I bet she didn't even bother looking. We get a new Bear Bear out of the drawer, and quietly introduce him. He's accepted. Now there's only one back-up.

Two weeks later, we lose another. It's my fault this time. We're down to the final one.

He lasts three months, but then he's lost. She begins screaming at night again.

I go to Hamleys. No bears left. And there aren't even any in the warehouse. I give the Customer Services guys a picture of Grace and Bear Bear together. We've got loads of them. They copy the picture several times, and promise to circulate the details. They've got a kind of Missing Bears Database. Hamleys and I are on the phone on a daily basis. For a moment, they're hopeful about getting one from overseas. We start talking fees. Drop-off points. But then the hopes are dashed.

By now Grace is old enough to talk. She's got an intelligent, inquisitive manner. She's like a tiny detective. She keeps saying: 'Where Bear Bear, Daddy?' And at first I just change the subject. But after a while I can't resist it. She says, 'Where Bear Bear, Daddy?' and I say: 'Well, you know how he likes fighting. *Well* ... Bear Bear has flown off on the back of a Big Duck. And he's flown all the way to the land of snow, where he's found his cousin, the Snow Bear. And they're doing some fighting together, against some very naughty penguins.'

She says: 'Where Bear Bear, Daddy?'

I tell her about the epic battles between bears and penguins. I act out a very vivid scene, where the penguins are diving off the cliffs, and they're bombing him with eggs and pigeon poo that smells of fish, and Bear Bear copes heroically. He swipes the eggs aside with a big stick. She finds this wildly exciting. She finds this hilarious. I know my audience. (For a very young child, stories must always contain these things: (1) adventures of her own bear, (2) no scary characters and (3) poo. You leave out that poo at your peril. Poo is imperative. My mum gets very puritan about this. She says: 'It's not very nice. You can't be very imaginative if you have to stoop to the lowest level.' And I say: 'This is the highest level. These are the most imaginative poos you've ever heard about. Our poos can fly. Our poos go down the toilet on quests.')

Over the next two weeks, we develop a magnificent game where Grace asks me about Bear Bear, and then we have fun together telling stories. But at night, she's still crying. If anything, the tears are getting worse.

Then we go on holiday to France. One day, we're all out in the marketplace. Liv comes over and whispers to me like a spy: 'Look in that window ... Obviously we'd have to lose the stupid bow tie, but do you think it'll work?' I look. In the window, there's a French Bear Bear. I immediately see the problem: he's not fluffy enough. Also, the original was smiling; this French imposter, he is not. He's too French for levity. He exudes a palpable Gallic gloom. And he's wearing a pathetic bow tie.

I say: 'I think it'll work. Except this one's not fluffy enough.'

'Doesn't matter. Dunk him in water, so she can't tell.'

'Clever.'

I go straight in. I buy the bear. I ask if I can buy other matching bears.

'Oh no,' says the shopkeeper. 'Zer are no ozzers like zis one. Zis bear is special.'

'Believe me,' I say, 'I know that.' And before I've left the shop I've made my plan.

In the morning, Grace wakes up, and she finds a letter under her bedroom door. In great excitement, we read it together:

Dear Grace,

I've had a lot of fun fighting in the Land of Snow, but I missed you too much. Tomorrow night, I'm catching a duck, which is going to reach France at six o'clock. Near the rocky pier on the Big Beach, I'm going to drop into the sea, and then I'm going to *swim for it*.

Yours, with love,

Bear Bear

At six o'clock, we go running down to the beach together. I say: 'Oh, I think I can see the duck coming.' She looks into the sky. I quickly fling that unfluffy bear as far as possible into the sea.

She doesn't notice.

103

'Grace,' I say, 'he did say he was going to be swimming for it. Let's look out to sea.'

She still doesn't see. I'm thinking: See him quick, or he's gonna sink, or get swallowed by a big fish.

And then she screams. I've never heard her scream before. It's an incredible sound. She also flaps her hands up and down – a bit like Pingu when he gets excited:

'Daddddddddyyyyy!' she says. 'I see him. Swim, Daddy! Swim, Daddy! *Swim!*'

And in moments I'm ripping my clothes off. I'm swimming for dear life towards Bear Bear. And when we get him back to the beach we're so busy resuscitating him we're way too busy to notice that he's not fluffy enough. And that he's not smiling. But you wouldn't smile either if you'd been through what he's been through.

Over the next few weeks, she does, on two occasions, say, 'Daddy, why Bear Bear not smile?' The detective has figured out there's something fishy going on. She's following up a few leads, but she hasn't cracked the case. She suspects, however, that Bear Bear is not the same bear we had a month ago. But she's also taught me a lesson about possessions: things are only valuable if you value them. You must customize them; you must give them your love. I think she also knows that Bear Bear is not a real bear. But, despite that, she knows she loves Bear Bear, and she can see that we do too. What more does she need to know?

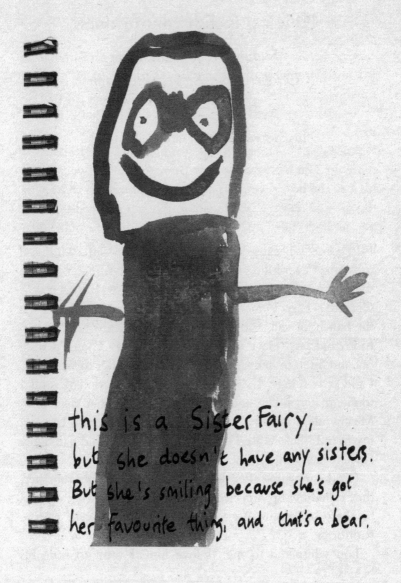

this is a Sister Fairy,
but she doesn't have any sisters.
But she's smiling because she's got
her favourite thing, and that's a bear.

Rule 25: Relish your madness

Summer 1999, Chichester
October 2003, Stoke Newington

'If a fool would persist in his folly, then he
would become wise'

– William Blake

I do comedy because of a friend called Lou Gish, who used to laugh at everything I did. I met her in the summer of 1999 when I was working at Chichester Theatre. In the play – Coward's *Easy Virtue* – Lou was playing my girlfriend. At the half-hour call, I liked to wander nude into her dressing room and say: 'Have you seen my clothes?' Then I'd walk out and listen to her cackling like a witch. After the summer, I did two things: I started doing stand-up comedy, and I found that comedy audiences are a lot tougher than Lou. Meanwhile, I introduced her to the funniest person I know, my friend Nick, who'd just moved out of my old flat. They fancied each other immediately.

On the morning after they'd first spent the night together, they called me up. I cycled straight round, and went upstairs to their bedroom. We chatted, then Nick went to the bathroom.

Lou whispered to me: 'I love him. I want to have his babies.'

I whispered back: 'I wish you'd do it soon. I'm hanging

out with people who I actively dislike just cos they've got kids.' I got an idea. 'Lou . . .' I said, 'why don't we take off all our clothes, and get back into bed, then Nick will come out, and he'll wonder what he's got himself into?'

She said: 'OK.'

Giggling quietly, we stripped and got into bed. Nick came out, and he saw us, and he stripped and we had an orgy. No, we didn't. He came out. We all laughed. Then I didn't know what to do. I realized I'd turned into the worst form of gooseberry: the gooseberry who gets into your bed and is in danger of squirting juice on your sheets. I put on my clothes, and went.

Then they didn't ring for ages.

Two years have passed. I've been phoning Nick and Lou, but they've not been returning my calls. I'm on childcare this week. I want them to visit. I want company.

The phone rings. It's Nick.

After a few minutes' polite small talk (Nick has very good manners), Nick says: 'Clovis, I want to explain why we've been missing your calls . . . Lou's got cancer.'

'What? How long has she known?'

'Four years. She had it in Chichester, but she never told you. She's just started chemotherapy, and is taking to her bed.'

'My God,' I say. 'Is there anything I can do?'

'Well,' he says, 'you could write her letters. I think she'd like that.'

I promise I will. I go upstairs straight away and sit at my desk. I decide I'll write Lou a story. I'm in good shape for writing. I talk to Grace all day long. I've got used to saying the first thing that comes into my head. I close my eyes. I try to imagine what sort of story Lou would enjoy. I wonder what she's really thinking about. I see her lying in her bed.

In my mind, I see two angels hovering over her bed. They don't look like normal angels. They look road-dirty, like bike couriers. One of them is a teenage boy with a big head.

I realize that Lou is going to die, but she'll be looked after.

I realize her story must broach that, ever so gently.

I decide Lou's book will be called *Dirty Angels*, and it'll be about that teenage boy, who has the power to fly with angels. I know that the book must have vivid characters – cos Lou's an actress – and lots of jokes. I immediately get the narrator's voice. He's called Colin Hitchin. He goes to the school up the road – the one where, at Going Home time, two policemen stand at the gates. I immediately write out the first chapter, which ends in Colin getting hung on the back of the toilet door.

I print it out, and send it to Lou.

She rings the next day.

Lou says: 'I love Colin Hitchin. You must send me more.'

I write an instalment every day. Every night, there's a cliffhanger, just in case Lou's thinking of checking out that night. Before long, Colin Hitchin is having amazing adventures, but his world is being troubled by a terrible villain, who's called the Master.

I tell Liv what I'm doing.

She says: 'What's the Master like?'

I say: 'He's a gigantic baby. He's forty-foot tall, but he can only be seen by people who are psychic. He stops people sleeping, and that makes them all go slightly mad. Then he can exploit them.'

'Are you taking the piss?'

'No. Everyone's got a novel in them, and I think this could be mine.'

'Everyone *has* got a novel in them, but sometimes that's where it should stay. But, if you want to do it, you need to make damn sure you sell it.'

Livy knows my normal system of promoting my work. I send it to one person. Then I leave it in a drawer to see if it can create a buzz from there. It's not the best way of promoting.

'I'll do my best,' I say.

'Great,' she says, 'can you do bathtime?'

'Yes.'

'Well, can you go and do it now?'

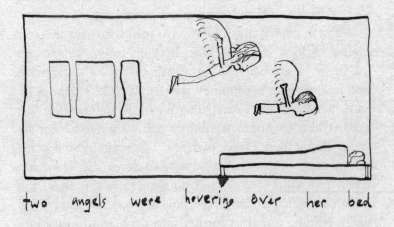

two angels were hovering over her bed

Rule 26: Spend less money, or you'll have to work

December 2003, Stoke Newington

Grace is about to be two. Whenever I come home, she never says 'hello' but she always gives me something. Sometimes it's her bear. Sometimes it's a spoon covered in yoghurt. It's a good philosophy: when you see someone, you must give them something; that way they might give you something back. She's becoming social. We decide to find a playschool for her, but we don't want to spend any money.

We're in debt as it is. I know two men who gave up their careers to look after the kids. In both cases, the woman left them. A woman will let a man sulk if he's just made two million on a big business merger. If all he's done is go to Baby Music, she expects that fucker to be cheerful. She expects him to make her dinner and to welcome her by saying things like: 'Hello, darling ... I thought you'd like a glass of wine before dinner ... now sit down and let me rub cream into your feet.' I can't do that. I can't be nice, and I can't be rich. In fact, every time we buy anything I feel we're pushing ourselves further into debt, and further into stress.

We discover there're two kinds of playschools nearby. There's a very cheap one, underneath the church, where all the toys are plastic and everything is a bit tatty. All the boys crawl around pretending to be lions, and all the girls are doing beading. Then we go to Mini Bliss Nursery, where you pay fifty quid a day, but everything is made out of maple wood, and the teachers are called Amy, and they're from New Zealand. At Mini Bliss Nursery all the boys are crawling around and pretending to be dragons. The girls, however, are doing something that Amy describes as a 'manual dexterity exercise'. It's the same thing: beading.

A manual dexterity exercise

Rule 27: Know your enemy

June 2004, Stoke Newington

I know someone called Holly who was once a real laugh at college. She was part of a gang I hung out with. When we were on E, she was the one who'd give out chewing gum. At five in the morning, when we were trying to get home from a party, Holly was the one who'd find a lift. She now has a three-year-old called Becky who actually says: 'Thank you *so* much for a lovely time.' The trouble is Becky's also got a scared look in her eye. And she never has a lovely time.

Holly used to have a good career in publishing. Now she's given it up, and has made childcare her work. She lends me books about parenting. Her favourite one is written by a woman called Dr Hilary Hoffenberger, who's a childcare expert from Birmingham, Alabama. There's a picture of Dr Hoffenberger. She's got blonde hair and a manic smile. She looks like a very Committed Christian, who cleans her body each morning with Q-tips. Her book is full of very serious advice like: 'When your child has a playmate, *teach them to share*. Suggest items they might wish to exchange, such as a wooden spoon, or an item of Lego.' You can just imagine Q-tip lady, looming over her child, brandishing her wooden spoon, and her item of Lego. That's enough to put anyone off their play.

So, on the downside, Holly is now so tense that, when you're with her, you feel yourself ageing. On the upside, she lives on the next-door street. She's got a kid the right age. And she's got an outstanding selection of Baby Mozart CDs.

That qualifies her, for the moment, as our family's closest friend.

Holly decides to send Becky to Grace's playschool. We went for the cheap one. The place is classic Hackney. It's run by a big-hearted Grenadian woman called Margaret, who greets Grace every morning with a smile. There's a friendly mum called Annie, who's always hungover, and she's got a gigantic child who upsets the other children, because she keeps hugging them. She's hilarious. There's a Turkish body-building dad, whose son doesn't really talk. He just hits.

There are several middle-class mums who are very worried about catchment areas, and security fences, and how the MMR jab gives you autism, acne and rabies. Holly is the queen of this gang. She is one of those mums who always says: 'I'll just stay till she's settled,' and then she hangs out while her child screams and ruins the morning for everyone. Holly is also chair of the parents' committee. She wants Margaret to do written assessments on the kids every week. She wants her to be watched, and so now all parents have to turn up once a week to help out.

The first time I do it, I'm paired with Holly, who spends all her time looking after Becky. That's obviously wrong. Rule One about helping out at playschool: ignore your own child. Push them away if necessary. Try to be interested in other people's. You won't be. But fake it.

The next Saturday, I take Grace to the circus for the first time. Grace is two and a half, I'm thirty-three. We're both tremendously excited. We've got cheap seats for the back of the auditorium, but we creep forward and sit at the very front, so we can smell the sawdust floor. The show starts.

We find the clowns tiresome.

We're not bothered by the sequined girl who dangles, by a ribbon, from the roof. We reckon we could do that ourselves.

But then six white horses run out, two feet from my daughter's face. There are five big ones, and one short one. This in itself is marvellous.

Then the horses dance.

Then they rise up on their hind legs and walk around the stage.

Grace is silent, in awe. Her mouth hangs open.

Suddenly it is the interval. We stand up. She clings to me. She's so stunned she's piecing the facts together, the way we do after a car crash.

'The horses *stood up* . . .' says Grace, 'and they looked a bit happy, and a bit scared.'

'Yes . . . They *so did*!'

'Are the horses all *right*?' she says, welling with emotion. 'Shall we go and check if their legs are hurt?'

'I expect they're having their carrots now!'

'They have done their work!'

'They *really* have!'

'They were up on their *legs*, Daddy!'

We move towards the horses' tent.

Suddenly I feel a cloud of dampness next to me. It's a bit like when you're out swimming in the sea, and then it turns cold. I turn and see Berky staring at me with her weird accusing eyes. Any second she is going to say: 'Mr Clover, I'm *so* glad you could make it.' We also see Holly.

'*The horses were dancing!*' Grace and I say at once.

'Yes,' says Holly, who has no time for this kind of nonsense. 'Anyway, Andrew . . . how's work?'

'Fine,' I say. 'Which horse did you like best, Becky?'

She just looks at me. She has no opinion about the horses.

'I'm worried about where I've parked . . .' begins Holly. 'Can you look after Becky while I go and check?'

I say: 'Sure . . . you check your car. We'll hang out here.' I put it brightly, but I can feel all the fun of the day draining away like air from a tyre. I want to tell her she can get a parking ticket any time, but only today will she be able to see six dancing horses, looking a bit happy and a bit scared.

Rule 28: Avoid TV. It will sap you

June 2004, Stoke Newington

When I was six, I used to pay my little brother 2p to show his willy to the milkman. I did that every day for a month. My brother started to make some serious money, which he enjoyed. But the milkman couldn't take it in the end. It's not every man's dream to be flashed at on a daily basis by a four-year-old. But I was experiencing one of the basic urges of childhood: I wanted to see how far I could push someone for cash. I got it out of my system. Some people don't. They go into television.

It's a Tuesday, 9.30 a.m. Liv still hasn't left for work. The phone rings. It's my agent.

He says: 'Channel 4 are making a pilot called *Balls of Steel* in which comedians all have three minutes to make a funny piece in which they do something brave. They want you to be in it.'

I say: 'Can I be the host?'

'No. That's not what they want you to do.'

'What do they want me to do?'

'They want you to go to the Norfolk Morris Dancing Festival in the nude.'

'Oh my Lord ... I really don't want to do that.'

'They're paying fifteen hundred quid a day.'

'Well ... I'll speak to Livy and I'll call you back.'

I know exactly what Liv will say. 'I know this is your career,' she'll say, 'but you're my boyfriend. You can't do that.'

I tell Liv. She says: 'When do you start?'

Livy doesn't care if I have to wrestle those Morris Dancers, as long as I get the cash, and get home to do stories.

The next day, Jason Hunstead calls. He's the producer of *Balls of Steel*. He says he wants to brainstorm the idea. I know him a bit. He's the sort of person who wears a tweed suit jacket with jeans. It's a look that says: 'Yes. I have an expensive jacket, because I'm successful and rich. But, down below, I'm young. I'm still ready for action.' There's nothing wrong with that look, as such – I've worn it myself – but it's also like the *uniform* for the creative person.

I say: 'Once I am nude, doesn't the tension quickly wear off? How about if ... every week, I am a mad personal trainer, who gives increasingly bizarre advice? I'll take people on the tube, and I'll make them announce every stop – "St JAMES'S PARK!" – in a loud voice, and THEN I'll strip, and try to get everyone to join in. Someone would try to kill me. But it would be hilarious.'

He says: 'Andrew ... Channel 4 want you nude, all the time. People might be flicking channels.'

I give him my real objection. 'Listen. I'd be scared.'

He says: 'Don't worry. We'll protect you. We'll turn you into a star.'

'Jason, if you're staying the weekend with someone posh, and you load the dishwasher, someone will *invariably* say: "Oh thanks. You're *such* a star!" A star is someone who does a task that no one else wants. I'm not doing this to be a star. Anyone watching, who ever had any respect for me, will say: "Andrew must be really desperate now ... and his buttocks are really gross."'

'They won't!'

'I went to see *The Blue Room*, the play in which Nicole Kidman took her clothes off. Did I leave the theatre applauding David Hare's witty take on sexual relationships? I barely reached the lobby before I started to criticize the shape of Kidman's buttocks. "What do you mean?" said my friend. "You didn't think they were fleshy enough?" "*Exactly!*" I said, feeling relieved my friend had seen what was so offensive about Kidman's buttocks. "She simply didn't have enough crack!"'

'Don't be silly,' says Jason Hunstead. 'You've got a very nice arse, Andrew.'

'Do you really think so?' I say. I feel reassured.

'Your arse will become a star in its own right. In a few months, it'll have its own dressing room.'

That snaps me out of it. 'Stop saying that! I'm not doing this to be a star! I just need cash, or my girlfriend is going to leave me.'

He says: 'I'll have a look at the budget.'

A month later, I'm in Norfolk standing outside a pub. Nearby two hundred sunburned people – dads, grans, kids – have gathered in a pub garden to watch the Morris Dancers. Hidden amongst the crowd are several camera crews.

Jason says: 'Take your clothes off.'

Trembling, I remove all my clothes. I feel extremely vulnerable. I'm thinking: It's OK, cos Jason is standing nearby, holding a clipboard. His presence makes this OK.

He gets a phone call, and wanders off.

Now I'm a nude man standing on his own outside a pub in Norfolk, which is not a place known for its tolerant ways. A woman goes by with her dog. She glances, and looks very angry. I confirm everything she hates about the world.

After ten minutes, Jason returns.

'OK,' he says, 'off you go.'

'What do I do?'

'You know . . . just . . . be funny.'

I take a deep breath, and I walk towards the Morris Dancers. I start to skip. I figure that, if I stop skipping, I'll start screaming. As I arrive in the pub garden, several grannies chuckle and point. Some mums pull their children away. But I think this is OK. I'm a clown. I'm a jester. I cheer on the Morris Dancers. I clap. Then I dance in amongst them. I whoop. I run underneath them. I jump. The crowd is laughing.

Now, you can say what you like about Morris Dancers. They love costumes and ritual. They love the Pagan Rituals of Olde England. They don't love having a naked man dancing amongst them. I keep skipping as long as I can, but one of the Morris Dancers hits me with his stick. I skip away, and keep dancing. Then the Morris Dancers stop dancing, and threaten to get legal. The bloke from Channel 4 cuts the cameras.

I run away, and dress.

In the car, I'm shaky. Riding back to London, I hear about another *Balls of Steel* stunt. A girl has just returned from South Africa, where she interviewed De Klerk, the winner of the Nobel Peace Prize. As he talked about his new orphanages, he didn't notice that the microphone was shaped like a cock. I really am no prude. But I feel almost winded by the sheer crassness of what's just been described to me. But it's good news. I know that there's *no way* this series is ever going to get commissioned. I know that watching the pilot of *Balls of Steel* would be like visiting a peep show to watch two disabled lesbians fisting each other. The spectacle would have its compelling moments, but it wouldn't be an experience that anyone would repeat.

A month later. My agent calls to say *Balls of Steel* is going to be a series. They want me to go nude, twelve more times. They'll use the best five.

The bare cheek of it

Naked ambition:
Andrew Clover in
Balls Of Steel

Rule 29: Play with your food. Talk with your mouth full. I wants always gets

July 2004, Stoke Newington

As a child, I loathed mealtimes. Granny's dinners were the worst. We'd be eating her lamb stew, bleached cabbage and soggy sprouts, and she'd be saying: 'Stop playing with your food!' or 'Don't speak with your mouth full!' or 'I wants never gets,' which is *terrible* advice. Imagine telling kids they will *never* get what they want. It's a manifesto for permanent disappointment.

But even the meals at home were bad. Throughout much of his childhood, my little brother stuck by his protest against the lamb chop. My mum is a Thatcherite: she would try to break him. She'd say: 'You won't get up till you've eaten it,' and by God he wouldn't. Sometimes, at 4 p.m., he'd still be staring at that chop, like an infant poet, contemplating an image of decline.

I learned to become a Big Eater. Other mums would notice this: 'Look at Andrew eating up,' they'd say. 'He's a *very* Big Eater.' I'd shovel the mince down my gob. I'd look around at the other kids proudly. 'Watch and learn,' I wanted to say. 'This is the child they love: the one with an empty bowl, and mince down his front.'

I've been thinking about this because my mum is still visiting to look after the girls. She comes nine days a month, and those are the days when I work. Last year, she spent the money we've paid her on a month's trip to Australia where she went scuba-diving and trekking into the jungle. That's the gran of today. She doesn't want to be eating cakes. She wants to be snogging windsurfer instructors. She wants to be shouting: 'It's always the way!' and she wants to be hurling herself out of planes.

Don't get me wrong. I'm eternally grateful to my mum. She looks after the kids with love. Better than that, she also does laundry. But she never really gets our views about food. One day I see her feeding burgers to the girls.

I say: 'Is this beef organic? Because cows are pumped with drugs.'

She says: 'It's not organic, but I got this from my Little Man In The Market. He knows where the cows come from.'

'I know where Keith Richard has come from, but it doesn't mean I know what drugs he's taken. And he's probably taken fewer than these cows. Did your Little Man actually throw himself in the way, when the cows were being injected?'

'They can put ketchup on if they want.'

I see there's little point continuing the argument. Besides, you've got to cut someone a bit of slack, especially when they're washing your pants.

Mum also disagrees with our sweet policy. We don't have any in the house. It's not that I don't eat sweets. I do. If someone brings a box of chocolates round, I'll eat all of them, straight away, and then, sickened, I'll curse the person who gave them. I know chocolate is bad for me, but I'm like a dog. I can't be held responsible for my actions. The body overrules the brain. But feeding chocolates to your kids ... I don't see the point, since kids don't want sweets if they don't know about them. We also don't give them gin. Nor do we encourage them to smoke pipes, or to trawl the Internet for chemical weapons. Grace actually didn't eat chocolate for the first two years of her life and, when she did, she spat it out. Admittedly, I'd just said: 'This is a mixture of animal fat, salt and sugar. It tastes sticky, and it will make you fat.' You might say this makes your children Fattist. That's true. But it doesn't make them fat.

My mum disagrees with all this. She thinks sugar never did anyone any harm. She's not counting Dad's diabetes. She loves feeding the kids pancakes and chocolate croissants and I let her. I love my mum's lunches, mainly because I don't have to clear up.

But I also love lunches when my mum's away. I've learned several tricks. I notice that many mums give their kids biscuits when they pick them up from school, because they don't want them hungry on the way home because then they'll cry. I think hunger is good. It's what makes kids eat boring foods. There is no child on earth who'll say: 'Mummy, no more biscuits for me. I'm now ready for a nice, juicy cucumber.' You have to give them the most boring foods first. So I starve them, then, as a starter, they get cucumbers and humous. We pretend that the cucumbers are shouting: 'No! Don't stick my head in the humous! OWWW!! I can't see! It's mushy and I can't see!' After that, we have boiled broccoli, and everyone puts on their own butter, and everyone pretends to be dinosaurs chomping tiny green trees. Then we have the main course, and we *always* play with our food. Sometimes we go for the Pasta Eating Olympics. Grace once got twelve pieces in her mouth. We declared that the World Record.

And I encourage them to talk with their mouths full. At Grace's playschool, there's a boy called Robert, who's the Walford Road equivalent of a Crime Lord. He pushes. He steals. He once got out some scissors, and cut off a girl's pony tail. Obviously, I utterly deplore that boy's actions. But

I definitely want to hear about them. The boy is an infant Scarface. So we crunch through lunch, and she tells me *everything*.

Infant Scarface

Rule 30: Consider the poof, and be wise

July 2004, Stoke Newington

The *Balls of Steel* series is starting soon. I really, *really* don't want to do it.

I tell Livy. She says: 'You're turning me into a cross, angry workhorse.' I realize it'd be unwise to agree with that statement. She's trying to trap me into some kind of syllogism. 'Look,' she continues, 'you have to bring in more money. It's just not fair.'

'Don't you think the kids will mind when they grow up and they understand that I could only get a job by stripping?'

'I think they'll mind a lot more if they've got nothing to eat. Do you know what I've done this week? I wrote a thirty-page Annual Report, which no one will ever read. My boss crossed out every other word, and told me to do it again. This job is your Annual Report.'

I agree to do the series, but it pains me. I simply can't see why it's funny. Eric Morecambe was never so desperate for a laugh that he had to get his cock out. I'm yearning desperately to be someone else. As my children soar through the air on the finest swings in London, I try to imagine how Peter Cook would handle The Naked Man. I reckon he'd be like a deluded innocent, always hoping other people will go nude with him. I see it'll only be funny if there's tension. I realize that, as The Naked Man, I must keep up a manic cheerfulness while I'm walking around, *naked*, waiting to be attacked.

I get hold of some grass. But it's hard to find the kind of

light-hearted stuff that we used to giggle over at college. I buy genetically reinforced skunk. That evening, Jason calls.

We're on for tomorrow.

I meet Jason at 7 a.m. In the car, I eat skunk. A lot of it.

I go to Battle in Sussex, where I have to strip outside Woolworths. I do a funny interview with a local butcher, who tells me about the pigs he uses for his sausages.

Two days later, I go to the Dorset Steam Fair, in the Nude, and some Steam Enthusiasts chase me, throwing stones. I'm finally pursued from the grounds by a fat farmer holding a stick.

I go to the Appleby Horse Fair, England's biggest gathering of Romany Gypsies. We drive to the middle of the fair, and we visit the caravan of a revered Romany Elder, who's running the event. He says: 'Two people died here last year. The police investigated, but they found nothing. If you get your tadger out, someone will bury you under that ploughed field.' It's not clear if his objections are moral, or artistic, but I get the message.

When I'm not working, I'm feeling tense. I start feeling a sense of shame that's as corrosive as cancer. Livy tells me I'm being grumpy like my dad. So I start smoking the weed whenever I'm doing childcare. If Livy's around, I have extra.

The girls and I spend a couple of majestic weeks of play.

We make up a story about The Four Sad Horses, who are called Apple, Dapple, Barry and Plod. The Four Sad Horses are us, in disguise. I'm Barry. I'm a huge black horse with hairy hooves. We improvise plays about the horses. One of them lasts three hours.

So I'm OK when I'm hiding from reality.

But Jason keeps calling to arrange more Naked assignments. It's like having a pimp. I go nude in Cumbria. I go nude in Central Manchester. I'm being a professional. I'm smoking a lot, and I'm getting through this. Yes, my memory is screwed . . .

It's 6.30 p.m. I've just come home from another Nude Day. I was cycling around Central London in the nude. It was quite fun, apart from the bit when I was arrested.

Back home, Livy sends me out to the shop to buy milk. Twenty minutes later, I'm standing in the newsagent's thinking: I MUST have needed something. I buy some crayons, some squeezy honey and some cod. I come home, and Liv greets me at the door looking like Nurse Ratched from *One Flew Over the Cuckoo's Nest*. She says: 'Aren't you supposed to be in Farnham?'

She's right.

I've got a gig tonight. I've got a booking to do stand-up comedy: a headlining set, forty minutes, for a fee of one hundred quid. I'm not going to receive The Naked Man cash for ages; this will be my only earnings this month.

I hand over the groceries and drive to Farnham.

I park in a car park outside, and look mournfully at the club. I don't feel ready to perform comedy. I don't know that I'm funny. I don't know I've ever been funny. I smoke a large joint.

I go into the club. It's packed. At the back is a terrifying mob of lads in Ben Sherman shirts. They're talking about cars. One of them says to the other: 'YOU are a fucking poof!' and everyone laughs. I realize I won't be able to connect with this audience. I also realize that the MC is the booker of the gig. He books hundreds of gigs. He's one of the most important people in my life. The compère sees me. He says: 'This guy is one of our favourite acts. Please give a big hand for . . . Andrew Clover!'

I come onstage, and I do what I always do: I say the first lines on auto-pilot. The audience laugh. I start a routine.

Now something very weird happens.

Suddenly, I feel like it's someone else who's onstage talking. He's doing an imitation of a squirrel that's on crack. The audience are laughing like it's the funniest thing they've ever heard.

This carries on for ages. That guy onstage does most of my set, although he misses out the middle of most of the routines, so they don't make sense. The audience doesn't care. They're wetting themselves with laughter. The man gets off. The audience applauds loudly.

The man steps off the stage.

Bang. Suddenly I'm back in my body.

The MC says: 'You only did twenty-five minutes. Do you want to do an encore?'

I think fast. I know I've got loads of material that I've missed out, but I can't for the life of me remember what it is. I say, a little too emphatically: 'I've *got to go* ... I've **got** to go home.'

I go.

Half an hour later, I'm on the motorway, and suddenly it's like the dream I had when I was a child: the one where I was driving a car, while not knowing what I was doing.

I am vaguely aware that this is dangerous. I try to work out how to drive. I see a sign by the road. It says 70. I see the number 70 on a dial in front of me. I make sure that the little arrow is touching the 70. That seems significant.

I pass another sign. It says 'London'. I don't know where London is, or what, but it sounds like somewhere I would go. I drive towards London.

Amazingly, I make it home. Safe in my bedroom, I see it's 2 a.m. I go straight to bed. I'm doing childcare in five hours.

The next day. Ten p.m. I'm standing at Stansted Airport with my family and Gary. Tomorrow my brother is getting married to a girl from Cork, and we're all going to cheer him on. The girls are asleep in the double buggy. Livy leaves us queuing. She's gone off to buy some Essential Lady Items. I'm left alone with Gary, and I decide I'll talk to him.

Gary is an ideal friend. He's forgiving, he works in comedy and he's gay, which means there's little chance I'll ever have to play with his children. He's a hilarious peacock of a man. He's got a blond Mohican. He's got an enormous Irish water spaniel, who has a blond Mohican too. You know the *Little Britain* character of the Antipodean masseur who says, 'Just relax . . . and imagine a herd of stampeding bison.' That character is based on Gary. He's South African. He speaks in a soft, seductive voice. He's very liberated. He describes himself as either homosexual, bisexual or poly-sexual, which means he'll take anyone, as long as they didn't go to university.

I decide to ask Gary's advice, because I know it'll be advice I want to hear. I explain what I've been up to.

He says: 'Andrew, if you don't know where London is, *or what*, you shouldn't be driving a vehicle. I know what the trouble is. You've left your body. I'm gonna put you back inside.'

'How?' I say. It actually sounds like Gary is proposing to bum me.

'This works best on the heath under some trees,' says Gary. 'But we can try here. Shut your eyes. Stand up straight. Take a deep breath.'

I see! Gary has mentioned that every Tuesday night he goes to the Psychic College. He's in their Advanced Class. I've always wanted him to show me his wizard powers. I see he's using them now.

'Relax,' he says. 'You're being skittish. Feel your own weight. Imagine you're like a tree, and you've got roots deep into the ground. You're connected to the ground. You're connected to your body. You're connected to your life. Know that you have *everything* that you need, right here, right now. Know that you're you, Andrew, and that's a wonderful person to be.'

I see that in my mind.

I have no idea how long this lasts. As a tree, my time-keeping skills are not important. But, when I come round, Gary's looking at me. I smell the aroma of croissants drifting over from a shop. I'm back.

'Is that it?' I ask. 'Don't I have to do anything else?'

'Be careful what you wish for. And stay off the skunk,' he says. 'You can give it to me if you want. I'm a professional.'

At that moment, we realize that Grace has woken up. She's staring at something, fascinated. We look up and see that *Balls of Steel* is being shown on a TV screen above the heads of all our fellow passengers. Onscreen, I'm jumping around, naked except for a woolly hat. I'm shouting: 'Go NUDE!! You have nothing to lose but your pants!'

Gary says: 'Your body is looking good. You could almost be gay!'

I turn my attention to Grace. She's rapidly re-evaluating everything she previously knew about her father. Then she screams with laughter and says: 'Daddy! You are on television! And you are NUDE!'

We all watch. I recognize the moment they're showing on the screen. It's the funny interview I did with the butcher. *Balls of Steel* have distilled it down to a three-second clip. My penis is flopping about, next to a chipolata.

Grace is still chuckling to herself several minutes later. She has a very infectious giggle. I get her out of the pushchair. She looks around at the dreary airport.

'Daddy,' she whispers, 'this is boring! Let's take all our clothes off and run around shouting.'

Gary and I both laugh.

'If you want to do it,' I say, 'you can. I'll laugh. But there's no way I'm going to encourage you. Why don't I tell you a story instead? Would you like that?'

'Yes,' she says.

'Well,' I say, 'there were Four Sad Horses, and their names were Apple, Dapple, Barry and Plod. Barry was a big horse with hairy hooves, and, every day, he had to go to work ...'

1. Stand still. Shut your eyes. Imagine you have roots.

2. Imagine the air is gold. Imagine you have everything you need.

3. Stay off the skunk.

Rule 31: Turn to God if you want a good Ofsted rating. But do it early

July 2004, Stoke Newington

Grace is going to be three in January. Liv feels one of the primal urges of the middle-class female. She gives in to it: she spends one entire night surfing www.ofsted.gov.uk to find out about schools. 'Our local school gets an Ofsted score of twenty-four,' she announces at 8 p.m. 'That's low. That's very low. It has seventy-five refugees. Seventy per cent have English as a second language, only six per cent are UK Heritage.' (Ofsted: the new face of racism.)

'That's ridiculous,' I say. 'Stoke Newington's full of clever, posh people. Some of their kids must be going to the school.'

'If they are, they must be very bored, what with everyone else still learning English.'

'I'm going to speak to all the middle-class people,' I say. 'If we don't commit to the local school, then we'll all have to move. It will ruin our lives, and ultimately it will ruin society. I'm organizing a campaign.'

'How are you going to do that?' she says. 'You hate phones so much you don't even call to wish your own dad happy birthday.'

I go out and smoke.

At midnight, I call in again. 'I've found a school in Acton,' she says, 'which does Portuguese. It scores twenty-eight.'

The next morning, she says she's found a C of E school,

two miles away, which scores thirty-one. It gets rave reviews. Faith schools often do. Christian kids read more books. OK, they've got titles like *I've Got a Friend in Jesus*, but they're books.

We go to church that Sunday. Whenever I go into a church, I immediately feel extremely ungodly. First of all, I scan for the sexiest woman. I usually settle on someone busty in the choir, and I home in on her, like a horny *Songs of Praise* cameraman, and I imagine what she'd look like naked, sitting on my lap. Then I glance around the church, and get cross about the expensive clothes. Obviously you shouldn't go to church wearing shorts and a paint-splattered T-shirt, but all those men in Richard James suits – that looks wrong. Isn't the idea that it's easier for a camel to pass through the eye of a needle, than it is for a rich man to enter into heaven? These guys seem sleek, rich and confident, like they've invested cash in a business that is producing miniature camels. They look like they've visited heaven, and they've bought a beachside holiday house. But why shouldn't they be confident? Their kids are going to a school that scores thirty-one Ofsted points.

I like the church, though. I like the singing. I find the prayers soothing. It would be lovely, if it weren't for the kids. There may be people who chose the church for its fine windows and excellent sermons. If there are, they definitely have kids. *Everyone* has kids. And I like kids. But, if I'm trying to fill my soul with peace, it doesn't help if there's some child discussing dinosaurs. I see one young Christian who's wiping his bogey on the hymnbook.

At half time, everyone leaves for Sunday School. It's *rammed* – at least forty kids the same age as ours. We ask other parents about the school. You've never heard such denial: '*What?*' they say. '*School?* We're not here for that. No no no. We're just very committed Christians ... Aren't you?'

'We're uncommitted Satanists,' I say. 'We're willing to worship Satan, if he can teach French.'

Back home, we work it out: the vicar must, at some point, be judging who are the most committed Christians. We've got a chance of nicking a place off another kid. But we'll have to get really hardcore.

We go every week. Wearing red. Singing louder than Pavarotti. And when we can't go, I ask the vicar if he can email me the sermon. This is the thing that makes me most embarrassed: during 'Amazing Grace', I raise my arms and point to the heavens. Like a football fan whose team has just stuffed the Germans. Liv does it too. I'm amazed at her. She looks like she might begin speaking in tongues. I start to feel fiercely Christian. I want to shout: 'Lord, come to us! And accept our daughter into that school!'

We sign up for the Prophecy Workshop. We reckon only madmen would sign up for the Prophecy Workshop. We hire a babysitter and, one Tuesday night, we go there as a couple. We can't believe it when we arrive. *There are thirty people there* – most of them, tellingly, in their mid-thirties. Parent age. It's horribly clear: Christianity is fun, but it's providing no peace of mind. The Lord can't guarantee a school place. Liv looks at the room full of shyly smiling faces. She says: 'Let's go and get dinner. Let's dine for Jesus.'

We go and have dinner. We've not spent time together in ages. Liv tells me she's heard of a middle-class paradise of gardens, and woods, and schools that score as high as thirty-four. It's a promised land, called Muswell Hill.

'Let's move there,' she says. 'We'll find the cheapest house in the whole area. And I'm going to stop my job. And then I'll spend four days a week at home.'

'What will you do with the other three days?'

'I've found out about a high-street fashion house that wants to have an ethical clothing range. I'm going to help set it up.'

'Do you think they'll offer you a job?'

'They already have.'

'Oh. Wow. Well done, honey.'

'It's not much money. But I figure we can sell your Harlesden flat.'

'I like having that. It makes me feel like a property baron.'

'Yes, but let's sell it. I want to have the smallest mortgage possible, so we can relax.'

'So no more church, then?'

'No more.'

And after that we don't go to another service. I do pop into church, a couple more times, hoping for a mid-afternoon pray. But churches are never as peaceful as you hope. There's always someone polishing the candles.

Young Christian wiping his bogey on a hymn book

Rule 32: Avoid kids in enclosed spaces

December 2005, Muswell Hill..
Grace is three, Cass is two

We've been visiting Muswell Hill for months. Liv has found a three-bedroom suburban house with shattered windows and mouldy floors. It looks like a location for a *Crimewatch* murder. It's perfect.

On my last day in Hackney, I eavesdrop on two twelve-year-old boys. This is the conversation:

'You are gay!'

'You are gay!'

'No, but you are *well* gay!'

On my first evening in Muswell Hill, I pass two youths skulking in a tree-lined pathway. As I pass them, one youth says to the other:

'I think the third act was flawed.'

This is an insight into Muswell Hill's freakish Ofsted scores. Even the youths are discussing film criticism. Everyone has pianos in their front rooms. Even the tramps have doctorates. And now we're joining them. OK, there's not much life. Muswell Hill is filled with lawyers and business people from Germany and the US – the sort of people who love England, but wish it were clean. These people don't want life; they want facilities. But at least you don't have to listen to your neighbour playing R & B at Volume 50 on a car stereo. You just have people installing new kitchens. You have to listen to the planes that fly directly over, one a minute. The houses are uglier than the ones in Stoke

Newington, but they cost more, and the whole area has been ethically cleansed so there's only one tribe allowed: the ones wearing Cath Kidston blouses and worried faces. As I'm walking about, I notice a message pinned to a tree. It says, 'CONTACT WWW.BNP.COM.' The next day I go back, and see someone's written on the note: 'Don't pin things on trees. Trees have feelings too.' I'm less bothered about the tree, more about the Nazism.

Liv has to drive to Alexandra Palace every morning, and everyone competes for the same eight places outside the train station. On two occasions she finds a note under her windscreen. It says: 'Why don't you park properly? You're a fucking c**t.' So people do get angry in our area, but they express their concerns in note form, and they black out the naughty words. If a pigeon shits in Muswell Hill, then he wipes it up with a tissue. Otherwise the other pigeons send him a note. The note will be lacking in passion, but the grammar will be perfect.

The schools, however, are magnificent. And Highgate Woods are only five minutes away. Also Liv gets us an allotment nearby, just by chatting someone up over a fence. And once you get used to the suburbia, you realize that it's all rather kitsch and mysterious. There are sheds. There are jasmine plants and lilac trees. There are cats creeping along fences. I've only been on the street a week and I get invited to the Scout Hut for the Neighbourhood Watch Barn Dance. I'm a comedian. You don't get opportunities like that too often. So I go to that Neighbourhood Watch Barn Dance. I spin every woman round that Scout Hut, and some of those ladies are forty years older than me. It's marvellous. I feel like a toyboy.

So . . .

It's a Saturday. Three months after arriving in Muswell

Hill. Liv has got another new job. As well as running an ethical clothing range, she's also in charge of the company's charitable projects. So she's flown out to India to see orphanages and hospitals and a tiger sanctuary.

This means that, back home, the childcare has become erratic. I've decided to visit the Christmas fête for the kids' playschool. I've planned to get lunch there. As soon as I arrive, I see my mistake. But Grace has already disappeared inside, and I know I have to feed them now or Cass will kick off. Muswell Hill people are passionate about anything involving children. Two hundred people are packed into two hot rooms, with hard echoing floors. Just to get in, you have to push past a car park of forty buggies, around which a massive queue has built up, of sweating, angry people waiting to see Father Christmas. Mothers are sighing. Children are screaming. Boys are sprinting past metal-edged tables piled precariously high with books priced 20p each. I have a feeling very like Road Rage: I want to run, but I'm wedged in. I feel under threat, but I must not lash out. I must barely move at all. A woman is holding a plate of cake in front of my face, and a baby is gripping my knee.

Breathing deeply, I move the baby, and make my way through to the café area. A woman, whom I've never seen before, says: 'Hi ... I've not seen you for ages!' I say: 'Oh, he-llo how are you?' and keep going, holding Cassady, holding Grace's hand, till we reach the food area. I see a woman wearing an apron and an expression you see at charitable events run by middle-class people. It says: 'Yes ... I'm now serving Marmite sandwiches. But at any other time I'd be in charge.' I ask to buy food. She begins a long explanation about how she's got sandwiches but no boxes. I can't hear it, even though she's shouting four inches from my face.

I've just been passed a Styrofoam cup of hot soup when my arse is smacked, quite hard. I turn and see a neighbour – a four-year-old girl who we know from playschool. She's grinning. I see she's throwing down a gauntlet. Normally, I'd throw the gauntlet aside, with a joke. With kids, you don't want to impose your authority, because, if you do, you must ensure it's respected. But I've rarely felt less jokey than at this moment. I say, 'I don't want you to do that again,' and I turn round. She skips forward, and smacks me again. I'm actually quite angry now. I've noticed that when kids find that I'm playful, they often smack me on the bum. I guess it shows playfulness; they recognize me as a clown, but I always sense something ruthless about it: 'He's weak; let's grind him down.' I say: 'Do not do that again, because it's rude and it will make me cross.' She smacks me again. She smacks me so hard she's probably left a Map of the World on my bum. Suddenly her mum arrives. I say, 'I don't want her smacking my arse,' and I realize I'm basically sneaking on the girl to her mum, and my voice has actually gone squeaky.

And I also realize, as I move away, that I've broken a basic rule of parenting: as far as possible, never leave the house. Because kids are like farts. If they're yours, they're surprisingly lovely. They remind you a bit of you. You don't mind hanging out with them under a duvet. The trick is to avoid other people's, but, if you can't, always make sure there's lots of space.

Rule 33: Use cunning to defeat your family

December 2005, Muswell Hill.
Grace is three, Cass is two

I'm showing our new house to my little brother Chris, and to his sexy girlfriend, Ali. She says: 'Chris, why can't we have this?'

He says: 'Babe. It's what happens when you approach forty: you lose your looks, you gain an extra bedroom.'

I love my little brother, but I'm disturbed by how he no longer looks up to me. He's been lording it around ever since he started going out with Ali. She's on the door at a fashionable London club where he's been DJing. Ali has a reputation for getting her kit off and dancing.

I say: 'Chris, why don't we play tennis today?'

He sighs. 'If you want.'

'We'll play one set. If I win, give me your Lemon Jelly EPs.'

'If I beat you, give me Dad's honeymoon suit.'

'It was handmade in 1959! It's more valuable than a CD.'

'Chill out, brother.'

Bastard. He's trying to provoke me, and he's already claiming he's got me rattled. I'm going to bring him down like a stag in the forest.

'Ask for something else,' says Chris.

'OK. If I win, you have to lie on the floor sucking my salty feet, while I lick your girlfriend's breasts.'

He's outraged. 'For how long?' he says.

'Two seconds. On each nipple.'

'*Man!* Ali's not some trophy!'

Ali smiles at me. 'You're saying licking my breasts for four seconds is as valuable as an irreplaceable suit? I'm cool with that!'

I lead him to the public court, reflecting on my problem. I must win. But my brother is a far better player than me. My only chance is to find a psychological weakness, then to attack it with everything I've got. I also suggest we have a swig of vodka before starting. I only pretend to drink mine.

Before I know it, he's won the first three games. He smirks. He's thinking: You're Sol Campbell; I'm John Terry; I'm the future. I'm thinking: You're Sean Wright-Phillips; I'm David Beckham. I may be past it, but I can offer a tedious, relentless accuracy. Besides, I'm controlling the media.

Ali turns up as he smashes two massive serves. They're just out. 0—15. He serves another. I stop and study the sky. 'Do you hear that? Nightingale!' I say as the ball slams past me.

'Do you want me to take that again?' he says, annoyed.

'No no no.'

Then he double faults again. Then he slows his serve, and I hit a looping return to his backhand. It's the tennis equivalent of the donkey drop. He scuffs it. My return clips the net and plops over.

'Are you not going to say sorry?' he says.

'Absolutely! Let's take it again.'

He realizes I've started winning; I'm also cantering off with the moral high ground. He loses the game. Now he begins playing with a grim fury that inhibits his natural flair. Now I'm on a winning streak, I pick the pace up. I serve underarm serves. I spin the racket and hit the ball with the handle. He loses the set 6—4.

I take off my socks. 'Guys!' I say. 'I'm ready for my prize.' I kneel on the floor before Ali. Enjoying her moment of power over me, she smiles and lifts off her T-shirt. She unclasps her bra. Her breasts flop forward.

They're not the things of legend I've dreamed of. A touch of blue Stilton. Tram marks along the bottom. And the nipples point outwards, as if her breasts were eyes looking out to the side – like snail eyes looking round a stone. But they're still magnificent. I slip my toe into my brother's mouth. I prepare to begin licking. Then I picture how I must look: kneeling on the floor, slavering like a tramp, with tennis balls in my pockets to obscure my state of violent arousal. And the thought crosses my mind: I have won, but I'm not certain I'm acting like a winner.

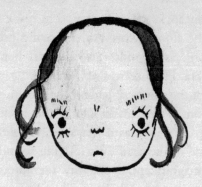

Rule 34: Gain control of the game

January 2006, Muswell Hill

Thursday afternoon. We're playing Cinderella. We play that every day. My daughters love Cinderella with a zeal that borders on cretinism.

'**I'll be Thinderella,**' says Cassady. Kids don't mess around. She's elected herself director. She's casting herself in the lead role. '**You be the ugly thithter,**' she says, pointing at Grace, suddenly spying the chance to settle some scores. (She lisps at this point, which I've reproduced. I've also put her words in bold, because that's how she talks.) '**No, you be the ugly thithter,**' she says, pointing at me. Then suddenly she throws up her hands and says: '**NOOOOO, you can't be the ugly thithter *you are a boy!***' as if I'd suggested the idea in the first place.

I see she's getting overwrought. I remember something from a book: 'Hypnotize them with calming language.'

'I'll be a boy,' I say, calm as a serial killer, 'who's *pretending* to be an ugly sister, because he is in *love* with Cinderella who's a *good* and *quiet* girl.'

She thinks about this. As a parent, I'm pleased. As a writer, I feel I've found a new twist on the old story. But then . . .

'NOOOOO!' she says again, hurling herself to the floor and kicking her feet. **'You cannot be a boy pretending to be an ugly thithter!'**

In a flash, I see my terrible error: I've presumed to rewrite *Cinderella*, the most sacred of all texts. I am contradicting the wishes of the Great One (Walt Disney). She would be within her rights to send in the tanks.

'You are thuppothed to be *the Handthome Printhe*! **Noooo!'**

I remember something else I read: 'Empathize with their feelings. Articulate them.'

'Cinderella,' I say, 'has it all gone wrong?'

'It'th all gone wrong,' she says, howling. Her tears are making a puddle in the carpet. **'It'th ALL GONE WRONG!'**

I do the only thing I can in this situation: 'Girls,' I say, 'who wants to watch CBeebies?'

Cass stops crying instantly.

We watch CBeebies. A little burst of *Teletubbies*, just enough to calm us. I think of Goran Ivaniševíc, who wouldn't go to Wimbledon until he'd seen that baby smile. I understand that. We all need to see the baby smile. Then we watch *Balamory*, which is average but luckily there's a lot of Archie, and not much Miss Hoolie, whose extreme niceness, frankly, makes me feel rage. Then *Story Makers* starts.

We're all hoping. We're all hoping. And then they announce it . . .

'It's a Blue Cow story!'

We all cheer. We consider Blue Cow to be greater art than Picasso. We won't let people in the house if they don't agree. I sit there and wonder why I love Blue Cow so much. Normal kids' programmes have proper animation; Blue Cow uses cardboard cut-outs, drawn by children, which are moved about on the end of sticks. The reason I love Blue Cow is it makes you feel you could make art yourself. That's what I want to do. I used to love art when I was a boy, but I stopped doing it since I was no good. This is an opportunity to do it again.

Next day, I take the kids to playschool, and then I go to Art for Art's Sake. I decide we're not going to paint on scrap paper. I'm going to get us all blank art books. And we're not going to use those £1.49 Woolworths paints that leave a grainy mess; we're going to get proper watercolours.

As soon as I get them home, we start. Grace wants to experiment with all the new colours. She paints a series of bizarre characters. I ask her to explain each one and she says things like: 'That is a smiley chocolate lady. When the sun comes out she melts, which she enjoys.' I write that down on the opposite page. Now she's got an art book, and it's got captions.

Then Cassady starts painting. Her art is more punk: she creates a series of princesses. Each one takes her about sixty seconds. As she does each one, she trashes another paint brush.

But I don't care. I'm doing two books, one called *Cassady*, about Cassady, and another called *Fun Things You Can Do*, in which I try to say, in child's language, how they've changed my life. We keep painting all afternoon, and, in the evening, we read our books. Some of the pictures are rubbish, but my kids don't care. They love the stories, because they're all about them.

Fun Things You Can Do

One day, Mum said: "let's have children."

I thought if we had children I would have no time for fun things like going to the pub.

Mum said: "let's have children."

we had children, two girls

Instead of going to the pub, we visit the tree nearby the pub, to collect Leaves

My girls like the ones that are dark red with brown lines

collecting leaves is fun

hoses are also fun

So is blowing dandelions

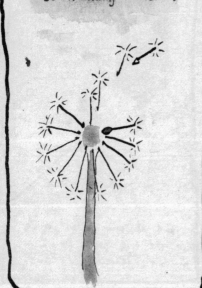

so is standing in ponds in

wellies, because it feels like The Friendly Pond Monster is squeezing your foot

if you want to enjoy a day you need a crown, fairy wings, and of course you must paint your face like a tiger

if you see a train you must wave

if you're lucky enough to find a bathroom light with a string. you must pull that string,

two or three hundred times

and when you're drinking on a hot day, always use icers, always use straws (the best straws go round and round glasses) and when you've

had the first sip, always go "hah!"

if you see a button you must push it

if you see an arch you must sing, to check the echo

if you have a bath you must:
1) use the shower to make bubbles
2) use shampoo to make mad hair
3) use the slippy end as a slide

You must read the same book twice. Second time, you must give everyone names.

an elephant called Malcolm Bennet

a worm called Maurice Clark →

Sausage dog called Professor Hamish Crompton the foremost Sausage Expert in the West Midlands

If you see a balloon, tell everyone

also if you see a dog with a lampshade on its head

and when you're really ANGRY and UPSET with someone

you should stop right away if they blow bubbles, or wiggle their ears

or tom on the television

I used to read books about Russian people who discover, after a long long time, that life is bad.

Now I read books about sheep who like hiding behind bushes.

Baaa

You can lift a flap and find a sheep. With the others you can never lift a flap to find a Russian

I watched films where men flew planes to exploding planets to rescue ladies with big chest bumps

Now we watch films about girls who make friends with fishes

these films are much better.

My girls are quite right. The car is much better with princess stickers on the windows

and the bath is better now it's filled with frogs, squirty bottles, and wee

without the help of my girls, I'd never see the magnificence of the world at 4.15 in the morning

my children are more interesting than balloons, and more beautiful than the red leaves with brown lines,

And they've reminded me of something I'd forgotten: there's lots and lots and lots of time, and so many fun things you can do.

Rule 35: You can lead a horse to water, but you can't make him dance (and everything you need to know about hosting kids' parties)

January 2006, Muswell Hill

I've got very strong views about children's parties, which is mainly because when I was a child I only had one of them. The best thing about it was the Deadly Fortress birthday cake that my mother made for me. It was basically just a round sponge covered with green icing, but I decorated it with plastic soldiers, who were mid-battle. I had some cutlass-waving Turks sneaking round the outside, but you could just *tell* they were going to be no match for the World War One Tommies, who were standing guard on the top with guns. The Tommies also had back-up: a squadron of Red Indians, who were huddling inside, ready to burst out.

Now. Let's get the facts straight. We were celebrating my fourth birthday. My mum decided it would be held on the Saturday after my birthday. Already, I felt this was showing scant disregard for the actual details, and I resented that. But the major problems really started because it emerged I would have to share the event with my brother James, who was two. His friends were only toddlers. Some of them couldn't stand up without holding on to furniture, and they wouldn't understand the games. I had foreseen the problems inherent with that, weeks in advance, and I'd warned my mother, quite forcefully, of the possible dangers. She stuck to her plan. She even invited a Family Friend.

OK. The day arrived. Kids turned up. They brought presents, although, confusingly, they weren't all for me. The toddlers all came with their parents, so the living room was filled with knocking knees and adults talking. It was noisy. Energy was high. We cracked into the games pretty much right away. It was Musical Bumps, which I won. Fair enough. It was my party, and I'm pretty much unbeatable at Musical Bumps. After that was Musical Statues, which I was winning as well. But then my mum, out of some prissy, liberal sense of egalitarianism, disqualified me for blinking. A *toddler* actually won, and I still refuse to back down from my opinion that that toddler, frankly, was all over the place like a madwoman's piss. When I was disqualified, my older brother, Robert – who had also invited two friends – started to jeer. I pushed him, quite hard, and he, accidentally-on-purpose, stumbled into the Deadly Fortress birthday cake. Quite rightly, I took very severe objection to this. At this point my mother said that I was showing off. I felt, quite passionately, that it was my birthday: I had a right to show off. She disagreed. She sent me to the bathroom, where I remained for the rest of the occasion.

I am an adult, and I've since forgiven my mother and my little brother, but not my older brother. I pretend to, but I haven't. I've learned that passions can run very high at a child's birthday party. I take a keen interest in them to this day. We always have parties, and we're improving the system every time.

We've developed these very strict rules . . .

1. **Don't invite the parents.** If you're inviting three-year-olds, you'll meet a mum who says:

'I've never left Stanley on his own.' This means Stanley's mum is a neurotic, cloying her child with her needy, fearful love. If she stays, he'll be the one screaming. Parents are like alcohol: they make the guests loud and prone to tears. Parents also witter about the Three Accepted Subjects for Conversation: 1) school, 2) holidays, 3) loft extensions. It's bad this is boring. It's unforgivable it's happening when you're trying to conduct Musical Bumps.

2. **OK, if you've got a toddler, you can invite three friends with kids the same age.** But don't fool yourself, you're doing this cos you fancy inviting your mates to drink wine and sing happy birthday. Good for you. But Birthday Child will see those toddlers for what they are: rivals. Noisy whingers who may steal their toys.

3. **If you've got a three-year-old, invite four friends from playschool.** That's it. Sure, I know you've got a gorgeous friend who lives in Bedford, and she's got two kids ... If the Bedford family come, they'll become Family Friends. You were a kid once. Remember what a Family Friend is: it's a freak, whose mum likes your mum. My Family Friend was a strange girl called Imogen Statesby who brought two Victorian dolls. She wouldn't even let me burn them.

4. **Don't let siblings through the door.** We recently allowed a six-year-old girl to Grace's fourth birthday party. She wasn't even invited; she just came with her sister. She shouted when she didn't win. I got kids to perform their party pieces. Small girls lisped through 'Twinkle,

Twinkle'. It was cute. Then the six-year-old sang – at *length* – in *French* – and cursed the present I gave her. Her parting comment was, 'I hope your next party is *good*.'

5. **Do the party yourself.** I've got nothing but respect for professional children's entertainers. They manage to control a group of thirty children. They can even control a group of thirty parents who are swapping stories about their Polish builders. But they prevent everyone from actually mixing. I think that's a bit prissy. Me and Liv always do ours together. She steps in when I get manic. When she sees their little eyes fill with fears, she steps in with Pin the Tail on the Rabbit's Bottom, or tea.

6. **Remember to have fun.** Drug yourself if necessary. Be silly. Be zestful. Don't just do Musical Statues. Give prizes for crazy dancing. Dance yourself. You'll feel like you're at a rave, in the middle of the afternoon, and you're a giant! Brilliant! This is easier if you're not being stared at by a mum who's discussing property in France. Or by a weird freak from Bedford.

7. **Don't do too much.** Settle everyone right away with an activity (make a crown/wand/birthday dinosaur). Then have four games (Pass-the-parcel, Musical Statues, Pin the Tail and finally a Treasure Hunt for chocolate sweets). Then do tea. After that they'll be bonded and high on sugar and will conceive games far more interesting than you ever could. Watch. Admire. Only intervene if a child is on the verge of death. And only if they brought a gift.

8. **At the end, make the parents wait at the front door. Carry their children to them.** Why? You'll feel like Superdad as you carry over the child, who'll be quietly inspecting their Going-home Bag. Introducing a parent, at this stage, would be like bringing in a wild boar. It would cause screams, panic and untold savagery.

9. **It also means the party will finish on time.** Your child can open the presents. You can eat the cake. Everyone's a winner.

Rule 36: Exploit your kids

January 2006, Muswell Hill

It's January, the month of rain and bitterness. We're playing hide and seek. I've been lying behind the sofa for an hour. At one point, a child even cried, but I stayed silent. I'm no fool. I'm reading an article about Daniel Gilbert who claims to have scientific proof that children do not make you happy. I don't know how he's proved this. I just skim newspapers. I get enough to confirm all my previous prejudices.

I'm feeling fat and old. I said that to my family when I last saw them, and they all went 'No no no no, *you're* not fat'. I don't care what they say: I feel fat, my hair is thinning and I feel old. I'm thirty-five, the age where footballers say they're 'several yards faster up top'. I'm not faster up top. My stomach is stuffed with chocolates. My head is clogged with envy and unfulfilled ambition.

I blame my kids. I'm so resentful I could sue them. I used to jog. I don't now. If I go out, I must bring children. Yes, yes, I know, you do see those uptight freaks who run pushing three-wheel buggies, but, if I run, I need encouragement. I can't be pushing a vehicle. I can't be stopping to pick up bears. And there's no way I'm joining a gym. I'm still angry that LA Fitness made me pay for seven months even after I moved house. Gyms are like smack dealers. They prey on people with low self-esteem. They give moments of pleasure, then months of self-hatred, for which they charge.

The kids are drawing hairstyles on pictures of Charlie and Lola. They demand my help, quite petulantly. I think

Lauren Child earns enough money. If her creations need new hair, she should draw it herself.

The kids are turning nasty. I drag them to Highgate Woods, where we play hide and seek. Then we run to the playground and we dangle from the climbing frames. Then I want them to leave, but they don't, so I promise that, if they come with me to the field, I'll throw them both in the air, ten times each.

We leave. We go to the big field in the middle of High-gate Woods. I fling both children. Child-flinging is one of the most satisfying things you can do. If you do it wrong, you can damage your back, or drop them. But if you do it well, you can get them to soar nine feet into the sky. It also provides an intense workout for thighs, back and shoulders.

They love it. But afterwards they both cry. I know why. They want me to carry them home. Normally, I refuse, since I'm training them to walk. But today I say:

'What's the matter?'

'We're tired, Daddy!' says Grace accusingly. 'Tired!'

The sun comes out. It's one of those rare moments of winter sunshine.

'Does it look a long, long way to get home?'

'Yes, it does,' says Grace. She looks at me suspiciously. She's expecting more opposition than this.

'Does it look like the field is an ENORMOUS desert, and you're never going to be able to cross it?'

'Yes, it does!' says Grace, tears stopping altogether. Even Cass stops.

'Well?' I say. 'What must you do, if you have to walk across an enormous desert?'

They think for a moment. Grace remembers a game we had in Norfolk, last summer, where we pretended we had a Magic Camel.

'Shall we get a Magic Camel?' she asks tentatively.

'Exactly! Let's call a Camel to take you home. Right! Who can sing: "Magic Tree! Umerlamel Find a Camel!"'

They both start chanting: 'Magic Tree! Umerlamel Find a Camel!'

'Where is the camel?' I shout, looking around. 'I think you have to sing louder!'

They chant more. 'Umerlamel! Find a Camel!'

I make a camel face, and I do that weird groaning sound that camels make.

'Daddy,' shouts Grace, 'the camel is YOU!'

'Quick!' I shout, in my camel voice. 'You'd better climb on!'

I put Cass on my shoulders, since she likes to be Look Out. I hold Grace in my arms, since she likes to chat.

'I could be the Blue Witch,' says Grace.

'**And I am Princess Lavender,**' says Cass, '**and you are the Camel.**' She wants to make *damn* sure of that. We all plod home slowly. Cass looks for squirrels. Grace and I make up a long story about a princess who lives in the desert.

As soon as we are back in the house, Cass fetches a blonde wig. '**You are not the Camel any more,**' she reassures me. '**You are Princess Velvet. And you're a beeeeaufitul lady and you've got white hair.**'

She passes the wig. I put it on. I immediately feel luscious and ladylike and beeeeeaufitul. 'We are the most beautiful ladies in all France!' I say.

'**No!**' says Princess Lavender. '**You are my mum! And I am more prettier than you!**'

'How dare you?' I say. This is sensational. I've read a hundred fairy stories. I've never experienced the jealousy of the wicked stepmother.

'**Right!**' says Princess Lavender. '**Then you must put on**

164

make-up, and I must put on make-up, and then *we will know*.' We get out the face paints, and apply rouge and eye shadow. I'm deep into character now. I'm wearing a girl's ballet skirt round each leg. I've also decided Princess Velvet has a fondness for drinking gin. 'I'm still FAR more prettier than you!' I say, slurring slightly. I'm quite magnificent.

'**Right!**' says Princess Lavender. '**Then I will dance and you will dance and I will show you I am MORE PRETTIER THAN YOU BECAUSE YOU ARE OLD!**'

'Let's just see about that!'

We put on some music. The dance-off begins. My daughters are huge fans of Early Elvis. 'Let me be yooooouuur teddy-bear!' That's a sentiment they can understand. Princess Lavender dances. Princess Velvet dances. The Blue Witch dances. Then we put on Bob the Builder, and we just jump. Then we put on Christmas Carols, and Lavender leads us through a contemporary dance piece that involves us putting our heads through our legs. She gets so carried away with her choreography, the dance-off is essentially abandoned. Then we put on Louis Prima and we just run about shouting. If I could tell the parents of the world just one thing, it would be this: get hold of Louis Prima's *The Original*. It's got a mad boisterousness that exactly matches the energy of excitable children. It's impossible to listen to 'Just a Gigolo' without moving wildly.

Then it's bathtime, but they're too manic to stop.

'Right!' I say. 'If you get nude, I'll fly you up the stairs.' They know the drill. They both strip, stand on chairs and hold their wings out. I give the usual choices: 'What are you – Angel, Fairy or Jet?' Then I do the usual preparation: 'Are you feeling light?'

'Yes, Daddy!'

'Do you believe you can fly?'

'Yes, Daddy!'

'Well, *jump* into my arms!'

Grace is a fairy who soars to the ceiling. Cass is a jet. I fly her round the house at speed, then crashland her in the bath. She says I've done it wrong. I have to fly her downstairs and come in again.

After that I do stories. Then I get in the bath myself, and lie back. I feel like I've run a marathon while carrying a three-stone fairy. I feel good. I think Daniel Gilbert is only half right. Kids don't necessarily make you happy. But Louis Prima does. And dancing does. And a man dancing on his own in wig and make-up: that's a freak. That's the murderer from *The Silence of the Lambs*. But a man doing it with his daughter, that's just Princess Velvet. And, I tell you, she may not be the most beautiful lady in all France, but that old girl has had quite a workout today.

Fly me! Fly me, you Bastard! Daddy said I'm a Fairy! Fly me!!

my daughter in thirty years

Rule 37: Teach her that there is no perfect man

January 2006, Muswell Hill

Sunday. I'm digging the allotment. I fling aside a skinny carrot, and my border terrier starts chewing it. I don't mind. She looks like a grumpy general, smoking a cigar. And I don't actually want to eat the carrot. At this moment, I don't think there's one person in this country who's saying: 'I'd *kill* for a nice carrot!' I like drinking carrot juice, though I find juice-making a bit like sex: I like it, but can't be bothered with the preparation, and all the clearing up afterwards.

Liv arrives. She says: 'Can you make boxes to go round the different patches?'

'Why?'

'It'll look neater. And James is coming round.'

'Who's James?'

'You know ... Lizzie's dad.'

'Oh! The lawyer. The one who always says: "Good morning. How are you?"'

'There's nothing wrong with that.'

'It's not very rock 'n' roll, though, is it?'

'I don't want rock 'n' roll. I want someone who doesn't frown in the mornings.'

'I see. So you fancy him since he does all the things I don't. And now you want me to give your patch a Brazilian. You don't want any unsightly weeds poking out.'

She laughs. 'Well,' she says, grinning impishly, 'I could talk to him about firm courgettes, and then we could hide in a shed and strip to our pants and wellies.' I laugh. My wife is brazenly contemplating adultery, but I find it horny that she's being funny. 'I think he might be the perfect man,' she adds. 'He knows everything about planting. You just want to leave everything.'

She's referring to my Brussel sprout, which I planted as soon as we got the allotment. The pigeons immediately ate most of it. She wanted to chuck what was left. I protested.

I begin sawing wood. 'Liv,' I say, 'what is the perfect man like?'

'He has a really good job, which takes him no time at all. He is strong; he never overrules me. He agrees my dad is a genius; he never takes his side in an argument. He never frowns. He wakes at 6 a.m. eager to do breakfast. He puts the toilet seat down; he doesn't dribble round the toilet; he always knows where I've left my car keys. He doesn't fart; he doesn't talk about football; he doesn't try to put his finger into . . .'

'OK. Fine.'

'So what does the perfect woman do?'

'She takes two minutes to leave the house. That's it.'

She snorts and goes home. Six p.m., I've still not finished the boxing in, but I go home. Liv immediately leaves to meet her gentleman caller. I find binoculars, and watch the allotment from the upstairs window. He seems to be lecturing her. Liv is grimly digging up potatoes. A text arrives.

'He's lecturing me about pesticides. Please rescue me. L X'

I reckon I'll let her stew for a bit. I drink a cider. At eight, Liv returns with some potatoes and begins cooking them. Some hair has escaped her pony tail, and is trailing down her cheek. She looks fertile and luscious.

'How was he?' I ask.

'A bit annoying, but he put netting over your Brussel sprout plant. It's grown leaves.'

We cook our dinner, and eat. It's a joy to bite into the potatoes we've grown ourselves. They are like our marriage. The skin is thin and slightly bitter. The flesh is very sweet. After eating, I return to the allotment to finish the boxing. That Brussel sprout plant is looking Gothic. It's holding its leaves in the air, like a dancer raising his arms. The sprouts are growing in the armpits, like bubonic bubbles. It's obscene, but beautiful. I'm glad we gave it another chance.

That is Mummy and she
is being a ghost. She
is looking for something
but she doesn't know
what it is.

Rule 38: Shop at ASDA.
It's the beginning of an adventure

February 2006, Muswell Hill

My girls are obsessed with fairy stories. To them, *Cinderella*, *Snow White* and *Sleeping Beauty* are Sacred Texts. It takes one hour to dress them while they reject all trousers, pleading that Snow White only wears tights. I want to call up Disney and shout: 'Listen, draw some princesses with trousers, or I'm sending them over. You deal with them.'

But then we go to ASDA and discover that, for £3.99, you can buy a packet of five pants that actually depict Belle, Jasmine and all the other cow-eyed trollops. Grace asks me whether real princesses wear princess pants, which I think is an excellent question. Alas, we're in ASDA: there are no princesses on view.

The next day, Cassady is so excited about the new pants she wants to dress herself. She sees the chance of showing off her pants to the town. She wears two pairs on her head. In the library, some older girls snigger — but slyly, like Cass is a bit special. So then I put a pair on my head too. Now people laugh openly, and we're all happy.

Harsh critics might point out there are *so* many things wrong with the image of a grown man wearing a toddler's frilly pants over his head. But get this: a lone man wearing toddler's pants is a freak. A man with a kid doing the same: he's a good dad. People smile at him. And I don't care who thinks I'm a freak. I take a toddler for a three-hour shopping expedition, and she enjoys every moment. So do I. That's worthy of a knighthood.

When she gets home, she wants to act out Great Scenes from Fairy-tale History. Her favourite scenes are:

1. The scene in *Sleeping Beauty* when the Handsome Prince comes riding by and he kisses Beauty awake.
2. The scene in *Cinderella* when the Ugly Sisters shout to Cinderella to clean the floor.
3. The scene in *Snow White* when the dwarves have just left and the witch comes to the door bearing the poisoned apple.

They're great scenes, which give important messages: if you meet a stepmum, run, before she poisons. If you meet a dwarf, do his housekeeping. And if you meet a handsome prince: lie down and let him rescue you. Marriage will ensue.

I ask Cass why she likes princesses. She doesn't mess about: **'They are pretty,'** she says, **'and they tell people what to do.'** She goes off and lies on the sofa shouting: **'I need a prince riding by. I need a prince riding by.'** I then have to ride my horse. I have to dismount, with loud neighing. I have to feed the horse a carrot. All this is monitored, by the way. Just because she's Sleeping Beauty doesn't mean she can't criticize the performance more harshly than any drama critic. After correctly feeding the horse, I then get down on one knee and declare that I've ridden my horse over valleys and mountains, but this is the most beautiful princess I've ever seen.

'Now kiss me,' instructs Sleeping Beauty. And, in that moment when I place my lips on Sleeping Beauty's ketchup-smeared face, I am not a man in his thirties who's losing his looks and turning weird, I am a handsome prince, and my kissing is magic.

Cassady's Art

that's a princess called Killerlo

princess called Pooberlilolay

a servant with jealous lips

jealous lips

Daddy is smiling because he's watching football

football

Rule 39: Accept all gifts
that life gives you

March 2006, Muswell Hill

For my first two days at playschool, I didn't talk to anyone. I watched. I noticed that the most interesting person was Gavin. I waited till he was playing on his own at the Lego table. I struck. I went over and copied, except I put an extra bit on the end of the wing. 'Engines,' I said. He copied. After that we became best friends, mainly because he was the fastest runner in the class. We used to joke that we'd split up one day. He'd say: 'You *never* make engines for me any more!' I'd shout back: 'If you're not running for me, you're not running for *anyone*!' But it's never happened. We're men now.

Gavin is no longer fast. He's a merchant banker, and he has a very busy schedule, which makes him tense, grumpy and fat. Last week, I invited him for dinner. Nothing unusual about that. Every few months, I email him an invitation, and he does as any modern Brit would: he only replies if he *definitely* can't make it. Otherwise he ignores me. But, this time, he says he'll come. I tell him to arrive at 8 p.m. on Friday.

So ... 9.45 p.m., Friday. I'm leaning on the front wall. He turns up in a massive Toyota SUV with sat nav, games console and baby seat. It's the full Vehicle of Fear. He's bought himself everything except happiness and a new cock. As he climbs out of the car, I feel a whoosh of affection for him.

Then he says: '*Man!* Your directions were *shit!*'

'Come in,' I say. 'Dinner's ready.'

We go in and eat the ruined dinner. Well, *we* do. He gets up to speak to his wife. I can hear him in the hall saying '*Babe ... babe ...*' in high pleading tones. I call this his bubble-wrap voice. It's a voice designed to prevent damage.

He comes back. I ask him how he is. He says he's knackered cos he gets up at 6 a.m. every day for work. And he says he's hired five different nannies in the last year, but he's had to fire them all. Then he says he's got to go since the whole family is going snowboarding in the morning. I *want* to say: 'Why don't you *not* go? And why don't you sleep in, and then wake up and *play* with your kids like it's the last day on earth?' I don't say that. I'm his oldest friend. I prefer to communicate through hints and sarcasm.

I say: 'Well, I hope you enjoy the trip ... I hate planes.'

He says: '*Why?*' Suddenly, he's really offended. It's like he's the spokesman for the Air Aviation Authority.

I say: 'I hate the pollution. I hate the noise of them flying over. I hate going on them myself cos I always end up at check-in at four in the morning with Liv saying, "Just *walk* to the front of the queue!" and everyone staring at the kids like they're bombs that are definitely going to go off.'

I'm expecting him to rise to this. He knows I'm right, but I reckon he'll do what any modern Brit would: he'll concentrate on proving I'm a hypocrite. But he crumbles like a wet sandcastle. He says: 'Don't give me a hard time. I need a break.'

I say: 'I hope it's fun. Send my love to the family.'

I hug him. He goes.

And for my birthday he gives me a Ryanair voucher for three hundred quid, and an open invitation to stay in his holiday home in Portugal. The bastard.

Rule 40: Love God's little creatures

March 2006, Muswell Hill.
Grace is four, Cass is two

As I walk up the garden path, Grace slams open the door. '*Daddy!*' she shouts, wildly excited. 'I've got NITS!' She runs back inside.

I hang up my coat feeling angry. It's like when they get colds: I blame the lazy parents who sent their kids to school with big green snot worms on their faces. This is even worse than a cold. My beautiful daughter is infested like a tramp.

I come into the living room where Liv is pouring stuff on their heads. I look at the bottle. It's called Nitty Gritty, an 'Aromatherapy Head Lice Solution – made by mums!' I read the ingredients. It's a mixture of oils – grapeseed, wheatgerm and lavender. 'Is this going to kill the nits,' I say, 'or give them a lovely massage?'

Then I give Liv a kiss. As I lean in, I wonder if she's got them too. 'Don't be cynical,' she whispers. 'I don't want Grace to think this is a bad thing.' I should have anticipated this. As soon as a development occurs in our house, it's subjected to spin and counter-spin. Last week, Val's cat died, but we, apparently, agreed to say that the cat had 'gone to live by the seaside'. At breakfast, Grace asked me if I thought the cat was now getting lots of fish. 'If she is,' I said, 'she'll have trouble eating them, since she's dead.' Admittedly, this was tactless and clumsy, but I was, at the time, dealing with Cassady, who was eating Weetabix, and she was telling me she wanted '**the TINY spoon, not the LITTLE spoon,** the TINY spoon, and you've given me TOO MUCH MILK.'

'Do you want me to check you?' I ask Liv. She refuses. She says she doesn't care if she's swarming with them; she's just spent forty quid on getting her hair done and she's being photographed in the morning. I'm suddenly feeling very itchy, but then I'm powerfully psychosomatic. As soon as I hear about a medical condition, I suffer from it. Last week I had arthritis, thrush and a mild stroke.

When Liv has finished the children, I ask her to check me. She looks for three seconds. 'You couldn't have them,' she pronounces, 'your hair is too thin.' This is an outrageous slur. My hairline has gone a bit Jack Nicholson, but I've still got a full head of hair. And my scalp is really itching. I scratch, and immediately find a creature under my fingernail, which waves a jaunty arm at me like it wants to make friends.

'Look!' I say triumphantly 'I've got one! Now please do me too!'

And she does. And I must say she does it very nicely. She rubs in the oil. She combs it through gently. She even gives my scalp a little rub. I understand why monkeys do this every day. I feel cared for. I have changed my whole attitude to the nits. If any more of them visit, I shall welcome them in. I shall feed them Weetabix and I will keep changing spoons till I find the exact one they like.

Half Hairy Mary.
She is missing half her hair
because the nits ate it. But
she's happy because she's got
a really good hat.

Rule 41: When in Rome ... get sunglasses and a Fiat, and drive around looking for toilets

March 2006, Muswell Hill

Cassady is nearly three. I love her, but she causes ruptions. It's partly because Cass had a nanny for six months, and Elsa would rock her to sleep every night. Cass learned you can't sleep unless someone's rocking you. Now she wakes up three times a night, and Liv goes in to pat her head, and I lie in bed saying: 'If you keep patting her head, she's going to keep waking.' This leads to tension.

Cass is good at playing quietly on her own. But she also has a firm legal mind, and a vigorous instinct for pointing out where her rights are being infringed. She punishes with spectacular tantrums. If you give her lunch, she says: **'BUT you have NOT given me my Fimbles cup!'** You get the Fimbles cup, she says: **'But I do not want orange I want APPLE!'** She bitterly resents my attempts to get her to befriend Jaz, who lives nearby. I'm trying to set Cass up with Jaz since I think she looks cool, and I'd like to hang out with her parents. Cass considers that an insult to her imaginary friend, Tilly. She knows that, if she befriends Jaz, Tilly will die.

So ... Tuesday night, 11.15 p.m. Bedroom.

Liv says: 'I've got a big day tomorrow. If she wakes tonight, will you go?'

I say: 'Or we could just let her cry.'

'Then we'd all have to hear it, and I've got to work.'

I say: 'You need to work. We need to sleep. She needs to learn to sleep, on her own. I think I can see a solution here. We put her in a separate room from Grace. We *all* wear ear-plugs.'

She says: 'But I've got to work. Someone's got to earn some money around here.'

I have a sudden fit of manly pique. I slam down the lid of the laundry basket. I say, 'For God's sake!'

She says: 'Why are you raising your voice?'

'It's the only way to get sympathy around here!'

'Cassady shouts, because she can't *talk* as well as her sister. And because everyone tells her she's a naughty girl. And because her own dad doesn't give her attention.'

Silence.

Next day at the playground I'm determined to play with Cass when she isn't tantruming. She's in the yellow wooden house on her own. I sit down. She says: '**Go away, Daddy.**' I go. I'm still a bit scared of her.

Outside the house, I watch two boys on the climbing frame. They're copying each other. It reminds me of befriending Gavin. I decide I'll wait for Cass to look at me. Then I'll stare into her eyes, repeat everything she says, and copy everything she does.

A few minutes later, she comes out of the wooden house. She gives me Leda, her dolly.

She says: '**Daddy, you must have Leda. Because she needs to sleep.**'

'She is a very tired dolly,' I say, and I put Leda in my pocket.

'**She is sleeping,**' says Cassady.

'She is snoring,' I say.

'**She is going hurrrr shhhhh.**'

'Hurrrr shhhhh.'

She giggles. I giggle. We both snore even louder. We become very vigorous sleeping dollies. Then we run about snoring. Then we run to the sandpit and kick our feet in the air like sleeping dollies on a mad piss-up. She stares into my eyes and giggles. I stare into hers and roar with laughter. I can't say it stops all tantrums dead. But it is fun. And ever since we've been much better friends. She's also started talking to Jaz.

Rule 42: Always be positive

1976, Luxembourg. March 2006,
Muswell Hill

I am six. Me and my brothers are watching *It's a Knockout*. My dad's on his sofa at the other end of the room. My elder brother says a word that's derogatory about the French. He calls them 'wankers'. Suddenly my dad springs from the sofa, and smacks him round the head. Hard. He says: 'Don't you ever swear again. You're a very bad boy.'

We're caught out. We don't think it's so bad to call someone a 'wanker'. Especially if they are (1) on television, and (2) French. We'd assumed that's the point of the French: to be targets for our gathering wit. OK, we think the word is bad, but not as bad as smacking someone round the head. But mainly we are surprised Dad has got up. That sofa is his trench. Normally, he doesn't move from it.

The next day, I have this conversation with him ...

'When I was thirty,' he says, 'I nearly joined the French Foreign Legion. By now I could have been a general.'

I stare at him. For a moment I don't see him as the man in front of me smoking a Silk Cut, about to pour himself another gin and tonic, using the bottle I've prepared for him on the SodaStream. I see him as the man he could've been: riding a camel ... shooting a gun towards an enemy fort. I prefer the second version.

'What happened, Daddy?' I say.

'Well ... I met your mum. I had you lot.'

I see that having 'you lot' – that's a consolation prize.

That's getting the peach-flavoured yoghurt. I know I'll never make the mistake of meeting a woman I love. I'll join the Foreign Legion. I am six. I think girls are for poofs. After that he tells me the story about how he grew up in the war. He had foster parents, and was passed around from house to house. He only lived with his own father for a year, and he was often beaten. It sounds extremely glamorous.

I'm thinking about this now since I've found I'm programmed to repeat my dad's parenting. The worst point of our week is 11.45 on Friday night. That's when Liv says: 'Who's doing breakfast in the morning?' My first thought is always: It's Saturday tomorrow. My job is to lie in bed till lunch. At that point, I must move to the sofa, to have a damn good smoke. I don't say that. I just frown. And then she says: 'Can you stop frowning?' And I say: 'Can you stop criticizing me?' And she says: 'I wasn't.' And I say: 'Yes, you were. You're patronizing me. You think I'm a bad boy.' And she says: '*What* are you talking about?'

At that point every week, I realize how I remember every bad thing anyone has ever said to me. All those criticisms – they stick in the brain like barbed wire. I also realize I've overreacted. That's why, every Saturday, I try to make amends: I get up, I fix breakfast, I sulk. That's my system.

This Saturday, Grace makes something over breakfast: straws Sellotaped to a sheet of foil. She can make anything as long as it involves Sellotape.

'It's a Wisher,' she says. 'You make a wish, and blow it down the straw. When the paper rattles, your wish comes true.'

Of course I could say: 'Look. I'm trying to drink my coffee. Now can you give me *three minutes' peace*. You're *such* an annoying girl.'

But I don't. I say: 'That is *beautiful*. You're so *clever*.' I've always wanted my own Wisher, and also I know that, whatever I say, she'll remember it forever. That makes me want to be positive. So I take hold of the Wisher, and I think: I want to stop being angry about my dad.

I immediately remember a story . . .

One day, when I'm seven, Dad does decide to spend time with us. We tell him we want to go out walking. We're crossing a cows' field when we see we're in a field of frisky bullocks. They stampede. We sprint for the fence. My older brother leaps over. He holds the wire up. My younger brother starts wriggling through. I fall on my knees and wait my turn. I'm terrified. Waiting to be rammed.

I hear a sound:

'*Stop moving in the back ranks!*'

I turn. My dad is standing to attention.

'*You! Call that a suede coat? You're a disgrace to the regiment! Drop and give me one hundred press-ups. I don't care if there are thistles!*'

Fifty bullocks are standing around, stunned by my dad's charisma and command. For that moment, he is a general. A general protecting his children.

Rule 43: Make them wicked

April 2006, Muswell Hill

I've been reading Freud who said comedy 'reminds us of the freedom of childhood', and he illustrated his theory with two hundred pages of puns about Viennese bankers. It makes you think that Freud must have had a very weird childhood. And his mum must have been a right dirty bitch. Also, if adult humour is about remembering childhood, it makes you wonder what children laugh at.

For young babies, there's only one thing that's truly funny: when a face swoops towards them, and then recoils. If you want a baby to choke with laughter, lie them on the floor and do press-ups over their head.

Soon babies are ready for the next level: peepo. You put a towel on your head; they pull it off. They're thinking: He's GONE ... oh, he's there ... he's GONE AGAIN! Oh, he's there!! ... Oh my God, does it ever GET better than this?

They love that. And they love being hurled in the air. And

they adore it when you pretend to drop them. Kids love to be slightly scared. A story is an excursion into the world of fear; a joke is the same thing, speeded up.

Now Grace is four, she's become a comedian in her own right, and she wants what comedians want: she wants me to laugh at her jokes. I'm thinking about this as I scrape scrambled egg from the bottom of a pot. I become aware that a trick is being played on me. These are the clues:

1. The sound of sniggering.
2. The sound of a child crawling towards me, being as subtle as a rhino advancing across bubble wrap.
3. The fact that two minutes ago Grace said:
   'Daddy, take the top off my squirt gun but,
   DADDY, you have to *forget* I said this.' Then she
   waved her fingers at me, like a very bad witch,
   and said: 'Forget, forget, forget.'

My assailant now reaches me, and begins squirting my feet. There are titters. I figure she's playing a game where she's being stealthy: I have to pretend I haven't noticed. But soon she becomes more wicked. She presses the gun against my buttocks. She empties an entire magazine into my pants. Now it's time for me to notice.

I look around the room accusingly. 'Hang on a second!' I say. 'I think I've been *shot!*' She is making this suppressed laughter, which is high pitched, and beautiful as a blackbird's singing. She loves it that I'm pretending not to have seen her. I put my hand in my shorts: 'What?! I've been shot, and I'm wet, and I've got wet pants!' She can't contain herself any more. She's roaring with laughter. 'Hang on!' I shout quite violently. 'You've got a gun. What?! *Right!* I'm going to *get* you!'

I run off. I get cushions. The first one I flip towards her. I attack with the next one. She attacks back. She's rapacious in her desire to hurt.

I run upstairs, screaming. She gives chase. This game has roused deep passions in her: nothing will satisfy her until there's a kill. I see that she's become a lion, and I'm a deer. I also see she won't enjoy it unless I fight back. Suddenly I snap out of it.

I become like a giant. I'm huge and powerful.

'Who are you?' I roar. 'You've got a gun? I will fight you!'

'And I will *fight* you,' she says, gathering her puny fists, and putting on her Fierce Voice.

Her first blow hits me square in the nuts. Fortunately, it's not too hard. But I groan and fall to the ground.

Her sister is next door. She's noticed that Daddy is being beaten up. She's desperate to get in on the action. They both jump on, and they give me what I can only describe as a Right Proper Bumming. They star jump over me, and land, bum-first, on my chest. I pretend to be dead.

Now there's nowhere for the game to go. And I've roused spirits so much that one of them will start crying. I need a bloody good distraction.

I walk downstairs. I get the paints out, and take my top off.

'You know what would be a really *nasty* trick?' I say. 'If I fell asleep and, when I woke up, someone had *painted* all over my back.'

I put my head on the table, and have a quiet doze. They paint my back. It's absolutely delicious. It feels like I'm being massaged by fairies.

they give me a Right Proper Bumming

Rule 44: Don't get scared,
get agoraphobic

April 2006, Portugal

So we've got this free Portuguese holiday, but I think it'll be too much hassle. Liv reads out the brochure: '"*Nestled in the fragrant hills of the Algarve, Villa Portofino is a short walk from the beach . . .*" It'll take an hour to pack. An hour to pop to Luton. If we stay, I'm going to work, and you'll do solo childcare.' I agree to the trip.

A week later. Midnight. I'm packing. Liv says: 'Have you got your driving licence?' I say: 'Oh God.' She says: 'If you don't find it, there's no point us going.' I empty drawers. I check pockets of bags. I visit the attic twice.

2 a.m. I'm so tired I've forgotten what I'm searching for. It feels like a metaphor for my life: I'm looking for nothing; I know I won't be OK till I find it.

3 a.m. I find the licence.

6 a.m. The alarm goes. We begin popping to Luton.

9 a.m. We're still popping. The M1 is blocked. Cassady is saying crisps are stuck to her leg. Grace is asking me to tell the story about the Princess Fairy. Liv is saying I should have turned off at the last junction.

11 a.m. We're in the air. I say: 'Let's look out to see if we can find the sea!' But a man's blocking the window with his *Daily Mail*. He's reading an article that recommends investing in Bulgaria.

4 p.m. We arrive at our holiday home. It smells of mould. We find a damp jigsaw of Noah's Ark, which, we discover,

is missing four pieces. We walk to the beach. The road is lined with half-built villas with metal sticking out of their roofs. The sea is cold. Cass doesn't like the squirly stuff.

7 p.m. We go shopping. The first shop has stuff an English person would never buy: Portuguese wine, Ritter Sport chocolate, bags of bright sugar almonds. This is bad. The next shop sells Frosties, baked beans and the *Daily Express*. This is worse.

We return home. I slump on the moist sofa. I've rarely felt so depressed. I notice the *Mail* I took from the man on the plane. An article says: 'The Maldives have coral reefs teeming with colourful fish.' I realize we should have gone to the Maldives.

Cass comes in. '**Daddy**,' she says, '**do you want to play March of the Penguins? OK, you can.**'

I am slightly curious.

I say: '*How* do you play March of the Penguins?' I go outside. They're both wearing wetsuits.

Cassady sets out the rules: '**I'll be Daddy penguin, Grace, you be Mummy penguin, Daddy, you are NOT playing you must JUST WATCH!**' She puts a giant pebble on her feet, and waddles over to Grace. They join wings. They rub necks. And then Cass rolls the egg from her feet, to Grace's. I'm stunned. They don't kiss, except in games. And it's an outstanding précis of the movie. I don't actually have a part to play in March of the Penguins. My job is to watch.

And I do. And I see that my kids know something that most adults have forgotten, except for the ones who write holiday brochures: places are only fun if you make them fun. You have to use a bit of imagination. And you may as well do that at home.

Me and Cass in Portugal, after I'd cheered up

Rule 45: Relax

July 2006, Muswell Hill

The papers, ever keen to relay bad news, tell me that autism has increased tenfold in the last twenty years. It's especially common in families where Dad is over forty. Great. We've mocked Teen Mums for ages. This summer was open season on Old Mums (they drain NHS resources). Now we can slag off Old Dads. They've had it too good, too long. Traditionally, women could breed to their forties; men could in their nineties. Like Johnny Vegas said: 'I'm in showbiz. If I play my cards right, the mother of my children hasn't been born yet.' But now we know better. Old dads have the wrong kind of sperm. The kind that stop outside the egg to count the other swimmers.

I sympathize with the autistic. They can't read emotions. That's not autism. It's maleness. They become fixated on rituals, numbers and patterns – why the autistic often excel at maths or music. They find the world unbearably chaotic and confusing. Well, so it is. And it's getting worse. Everywhere there's information, adverts, noise. Buses and taxis carry TV screens showing adverts. Roads are cluttered with signs. The whole world feels like one of those B&B bedrooms where everywhere you look there's a sign saying: **NO** SMOKING or **DON'T** LEAVE TOWELS ON FLOOR or **BREAKFAST** IS SERVED BETWEEN **6 A.M.** AND **6.15.**

It's especially bad for parents ...

Every day, I wake early, and always do the same thing: I calculate the exact number of minutes I've slept. Then

I go downstairs where I must measure out one cup of porridge into a bowl and two scoops of coffee into a pot. And I like to begin each day by studying the TV schedules. As I stumble from bed, planes are droning overhead. Next door, builders start drilling. If you're middle-class, it's probable that, at all times, one neighbour will be building an extension.

I must have coffee before someone asks me to do something. The fridge door is covered with paintings, Useful Numbers and messages reminding me of things I forgot two weeks ago. A child arrives. Wearing a nappy, a sock and a crown. She says: '**Daddy, can you untie my skipping rope so I can rescue my bear?**' Before I can answer, another child appears. This one's completely nude. She's shouting: 'But she is *not letting me* Use The Scissors!' I don't understand a single phrase of that sentence. Or what is required. Someone knocks at the door. A man called Brian says: 'I'm just here to measure the curtains.'

The phone rings. Like an *idiot*, I answer. An American voice says: 'Hey, Andrew, will Grace be free at four?' I'm trying to remember. My head feels like an ad break on Cartoon Network. Full of explosions. Barbie dolls. People speaking at *inhumanly* fast speeds. I just want to remember if Grace is free at four. Liv arrives and says: 'Would you please not leave the dishcloth in the sink because it really stinks?' A child shouts: 'Daddy, I've got a *sweet up my nose!*' I want to shout: 'Can everyone just *shut up*? I'm *trying* to concentrate on the *numbers*!!!' I don't shout. That would be mad. Instead I cover my ears and groan. I send subconscious messages down to my testicles: 'If you're making anyone today, make some of the quiet ones, who like sitting in white rooms, staring at walls. We need more of them.'

This much I've learned: life is hard, the world is noisy,

our baths are filled with plastic objects. I've learned that children refuse to speak logically, or one at a time. That's why you have to ignore them. After a while, they start coming up with activities of their own. Yes, some of these seem rather autistic. They go through magazines only cutting out the pictures of bags. They organize their hair clips in order of colour. But I don't care if they seem to have borderline Asperger's syndrome. I think: Relax; it's inevitable – we've all got it.

2 4 6 8 10 12 14 16 18
20 22 24 26 28
30 ~~32~~ 22 34 36
38 40 42 44 46
48 50 52 54 56
58 60 62 64 66
68 70 72 74
76 78 80 82
84 86 88

Grace did this. I don't understand it either

Rule 46: Always preserve your authority (it may be necessary to avoid confrontations)

July 2006, Muswell Hill

On Sunday, we take our daughters to an adults' garden party. It's a hot summer's day. They suggest we bring a paddling pool with us. A brilliant suggestion. There are four other kids there. Everyone gets in. They all get their clothes wet. They all have fun. Suddenly it's 6 p.m., and we need to get home quick, or things will kick off. So I say to the girls: 'Who wants to run nude to the car?'

'*Me!*' they both shout, and they run out dancing. Don't get me wrong. The car is right outside. I don't make them streak through Central London.

So they leave the party, dancing, nude, and two boys cry. One of them actually sobs: 'Don't let them go.' I am so proud. What an exit!

I feel we've created an image of happy, carefree childhood. I think: Parenting is the new rock 'n' roll. And it's so easy. You let them do whatever they want. Then they'll develop their own social sense.

But then today I am looking after a three-year-old, Sam, as well as my two girls. Sam is a very sweet boy. I met his dad fourteen years ago. He was living in Goa, making tie-dye backdrops for raves. Now he lives in Finchley, and sells organic vegetables. Sam adores coming round so he can be bossed around by two pretty girls. It takes Cass five minutes before she's persuaded him to strip. Maybe he needs no persuading. Anyway, he gets nude. I say: 'Won't you get cold?' He throws some Lego at me. I say: 'Don't throw things at me.' Cass throws some Lego at me as well. They disappear upstairs.

Ever since I've had daughters, people have said: 'What's it gonna be like when boys disappear upstairs with your teenage daughters?' I've prepared my answer. I imagine myself as a Nice Guy Dad, who anyone will confess to. This will give me maximum chance of talking them out of it. Failing that, Liv can threaten them. No one's asked me what I'm supposed to do when three-year-olds get nude with my daughters.

I figure that no one is going to get pregnant. I ignore them. But after an hour I have to check on things. I open the door. She is dressed in a princess outfit; he is still nude; they are arranging her bears on the bed, while talking in pirate voices. '*Shibbery timbers*,' they both say several times. He is also casually pulling at himself. Twanging it really. A bit like when you stretch balloons before blowing them up. I don't think this is really a sexual thing. He's just discovered that if you touch that area, it gives a nice feeling. Fair enough. This is something we all do. We just don't do it in public. Shortly after meeting our hosts. While their dads are hovering at the door.

I'm bothered that he's poking his finger down the eye of his willy, then handling our teddies.

Cassady looks up at me.

'He is a pirate,' she says. 'And I am a princess. You be a king.'

I think: No way ... I'm not joining in in a game with a nude child. Just say someone looks through a window. They'd see me with a naked child belonging to someone else. That's not an image of myself I want to project.

I say to him: 'Aren't you a bit cold?'

He says: 'No.'

I say: 'Captain No Beard, I'm going to dress you in these brown pirate trousers, and I'm going to give you an eye patch!'

He says: 'I like being nude.'

I say: 'Pirates were never nude. Too many splinters in their legs.'

He screams at me: 'I LIKE BEING NUDE!'

They both throw Lego at me. I've got a naked revolution on my hands.

I leave, and call up my wife. She's in a meeting with the CEO of a large company. We have one of those telephone conversations where one party has to do all the work, while the other person pretends they're taking an important business call.

Her: 'I'm in a meeting. Is there a problem?'

'Yes. Cassady's guest. He's nude and handling our teddies.'

'I'll get back to you by close of play.'

'I can't hold out that long. I'm not sure he can. He's pulling it so hard it looks like it might come off. Also he's throwing Lego.'

'You think the company needs to change from the bottom up?'

'I really do.'

'There's not much I can do from this end. But I would say ... relax. It's perfectly natural.'

'Yeah, but ... so's manure. I wouldn't want it in the house.'

I visit them half an hour later. I use the pretext of giving them mid-morning snacks. I give them some slices of cucumber. He eats one. He opts to wear the second as a kind of cock ring.

I say: 'You can't have food if you don't eat it.'

He throws the cucumber at me. I actually feel quite angry. I leave the room and take a few deep breaths. The problem, I realize, isn't really the nudity. The problem is he keeps chucking things at me, and I am being tentative about imposing my authority on him. I know I am being a bit like Sam's dad, who is one of those fathers who stands at the door pleading: 'Sam . . . time to go . . . Saaaaaammm . . . time to put things away!'

And then I remember what Cassady said to me when I first came into the room. She said: '**Daddy, you be a king.**' I'm one of those people who've spent their whole lives avoiding being authoritative because I don't want people to dislike me. I decide that must stop. Right now.

I march back into that room like a king.

I say: 'Right. I told you not to throw things at me. I'm putting your clothes on, and you can sit on the naughty stair.'

I pick him up, I take him downstairs and put his clothes on. He considers crying for a moment, but then he can see I'm like Clint Eastwood: I can't be moved; I can't be persuaded. I put him on the naughty stair, then I retreat to the kitchen and watch him through the door. I am a lot calmer now I've imposed my authority. The curious thing is, so is he.

He opts to wear the second one as a kind of cock ring

Rule 47: Don't give stuff, give attention

Christmas 1978, Luxembourg
August 2006, Muswell Hill

On my eighth Christmas, my brothers and I receive the biggest present we've ever seen. We save it till last. We take turns doing the Sellotape. And when we open it, we can't believe how brilliant it is – a huge train set with bridges, signals and everything. We say: 'Mum, it needs plugs.' She says: 'Ask Daddy. I'm tidying lunch.' He says: 'I'll do it tomorrow.' The next day we ask again. He says: 'I'm sleeping.' Twenty years later, I help my parents move out. In the cellar, I find the train set. Still without plugs. And I make a vow that, if I ever have kids, I won't give stuff, I'll give attention.

And it's basically a good vow. But whenever you react against your parents, you create different problems. You could rewrite Wilde. When a man grows up, he judges his parents. That is their tragedy. The man then reacts against them. That is his. I've discovered that, if you play with kids all the time, then they learn to depend on you for entertainment. Really, it should be the other way round.

The truth is I've had enough of childcare, and I can't be bothered with them. It's been two days since Nick called to say that Lou Gish has died. I'm trying to keep my mind off it. I'm lounging on the bed, reading *The Kite Runner*, which is a really good book. Grace appears.

She says: 'Daddy, will you help me make my turtle?'

She shows me some pieces of card you're supposed to cut out and stick together. I want to tell her the turtle isn't really a toy; it's a piece of merchandising that came free with her boots. I want to tell her that she must nurture her own creativity, on her own. I want to tell her I hate most of her toys. They're plastic and charmless and they take up so much space they stop us playing. I want to chuck them all out.

She says: 'I've got the Sellotape.'

I say: 'You be in charge of snipping. I'm in charge of sticking.'

She says: 'OK,' and we set to work. We quickly find the card isn't cut properly, and the instructions are inaccurate. I want to stop. But I know I always think everything is hard; I want her to think everything's easy. She keeps going. She really wants to construct that stupid turtle. While snipping, she says:

'Do you ever get cross with me, Daddy?'

'I *never* get cross with you.'

'You do if I fight with Cassady.'

'That's true. What's Cassady doing now?'

'She's put her bears on the floor. She's feeding them soup.'

'What's she using for soup?'

'Socks!' she says. We both laugh. Suddenly, the turtle's head falls off. Its legs are bending like it's drunk. We'd stuck one of them on sideways, because we couldn't see how else it would go. I want to stop.

I say: 'Do you think this will be your favourite toy?'

'Yes. We could invite Naomi round to play with it.'

Naomi is her best friend. I found out today that Naomi will soon be returning to America. I don't say that.

Cassady appears. She is carrying twelve bears in a pillow-case. She takes out Lucy Bear. '**Say hip hip for Lucy Bear,**' she commands. 'Hip hip,' we say. Cassady shouts: '**Nuffink,**' and chucks Lucy on the floor. Then she does the same with all the bears. I can't tell what the exercise is achieving, but I know it's something. A satire on fame? Who knows? It's distracting Grace. She gets the doctor's kit, and rescues the bears one by one. I have to finish the turtle alone in the end. I can't tell what the exercise is achieving, but I know it's something.

Getting Rid of Toys, Method One:

Make Barbie airborne

Rule 48: Remember – a friend in need is a friend whose phone calls you could be screening

August 2006, Muswell Hill/
Hampstead Heath

I don't know what the hell has happened to my friends. I don't have any left. Yes, I see a lot of Marek who can do odd jobs, so he's welcome any time. I like Lucy, who I have a laugh with as we push our buggies through the mental hospital on the way back from school, but I can't get my kids to befriend hers. I like Emma, who's the mum I fancy. We blush as we're hanging up our kids' coats. We find excuses to touch each other's arms. Thing is though: her kid is a whingy whiny nightmare who still uses a dummy, so there must be something wrong with her.

But I don't see my oldest friends. The ones I love. I never see David Walliams any more. It was easy being friends when we were both skint and bumming money off each other. Maintaining the friendship now I can hear him on the Jonathan Ross show, that takes a loyalty I don't possess. It's not been hard. I've had several friends become famous on me, and the same thing always happens: they ask me not to speak to the press, then they stop calling.

Most of my friends simply live too far away. They call me up sometimes and say: 'Why don't you all come over? We'll do you a lovely lunch.' I want to say: 'You live an hour's drive away. After that I'll need more than lunch. I'll need a massage, and you're going to have to dance for me.'

At the weekend, we do sometimes invite whole families over to play, but if you put two families together, there will always be two people who don't like each other. And most of my friends are single parents, or they work all week, so they feel too guilty ever to say no to their offspring. So their kids stand in the middle of our living room shouting: 'Mummy! You *need* to watch me dancing!' and my friends don't speak to me. They speak to their kids. And there's always someone who's crying, and I spend all the time fetching drinks. Then, if I get a moment to go outside and smoke – none of my friends smoke any more – then the last thing I want is someone else's jammy-faced child asking me to chase them. I'll want those kids to run off. But I'll not be chasing. Those kids will become a speck on the horizon, before I move a limb.

The person I really like is Gary, who's endlessly surprising and ridiculous. He's the sort of person who says: 'I'm feeling so energized and inspired,' when he's lying on his back with broken ribs. Gary only recently started walking again. He's bought himself a bungalow in the Brazilian jungle. He celebrated by falling off the fourteen-foot balcony. He also believes in taking all messages the world gives him. Last week, he went to a party where a man insisted that he should try out a website where you find people who want to have sex. Gary did. He and his boyfriend contacted a man who wanted to be used. They invited him round. The man arrived dressed as a gimp. Gary found the Gimp about as sexy as a banker's socks. He realized he had to send the Gimp away immediately. He did. The Gimp didn't mind. He thought it was a trick. That Gimp is probably still waiting by his phone.

On Monday, he texts me: 'I'd love a walk this Saturday.

9—11 a.m. Are you free?' I know it's selfish for me to disappear on the weekend, but I reckon that when making a plan you need to consider equally the needs of everyone in the family — kids, Mum, Dad. Who is the most needy family member? At the moment, I actually think it's me. I look in my diary, and see I've got nothing. My daughters, however, have three social engagements, three parties. I text back: 'I'll be there at 9.'

And I make damn sure I'm going to be there. On Friday night, I set an alarm. Saturday morning, I spring from bed at 7.30. It's desperate how excited I am about my two hours of socializing ahead. At 8.40 I'm ready. I've got my coat. I've done my hair. I've got some funny stories ready. The kids have had their breakfast. Sort of. I've turned on the TV to distract them. I've just got to bring some porridge up to Liv who's still in bed.

I hand over the porridge. I say: 'I'm off to see Gary. We're going walking on the heath.'

She says: 'We'll all come. It'll be fun! We'll go to the new playground.'

I freeze.

I suddenly realize this is my one social engagement of the week. It's scheduled to last two hours maximum. If they all came, it would take us *ages* to leave. On the other hand, I can't say: 'You can't come. You can't have fun. You cannot see the new playground.' Well ... I can, but I have no money. I have no power. Any objections will be noted.

I say: 'Let's leave in ten minutes. I'll get the kids dressed.'

I see that I'm going to have to work fast. I'm going to have to *help* them ruin my social engagement.

I run downstairs. The girls are watching their Charlie and Lola DVD. They love Charlie and Lola. We all do. Lauren Child is the great genius of our age. We all love the happy-sad trumpet music – Der derder *der*, derder derder *der* derder ... Trouble is: the girls have only been watching TV for seven minutes. Television, to a child, is like cocaine to an adult. If you have some, you're gonna need a lot. Half an hour at least. If you just have seven minutes, that's going to leave you feeling needy and incomplete.

I'm going to have to really sell this.

'We're all going to run about on the heath!' I say. 'I need you two girls to have a *running race upstairs!*'

Grace legs it. Cassady legs it. I quickly flick the TV off. Result.

But then Cass sees she's got no chance of winning the race, so she switches tactics: she bursts into tears.

Liv arrives.

'Cass is really crying,' she says. 'Has she eaten?'

'Yes!' I say.

'What?'

'Well ... she had a mouthful of Shreddies, but then they went soggy.'

'So you've fed her nothing,' she says.

Suddenly it's obvious to me what the biggest problem is in our house: Cassady has tantrums; Liv gives them attention. It's obvious to Livy what the problem is in our house: Cassady gets hungry; I've failed to feed her. Liv thinks Cassady is crying because I've ignored her, because I want to smoke weed in the park.

Livy makes Cass some toast. I sprint around fetching clothes.

I break the world record. In ten minutes, I've got them both dressed. I've even found the paper crowns that they want to wear. We've all got in the car, which is a miracle. It normally takes us half an hour.

But there's no sign of Livy.

I wait five minutes. I beep.

Another three minutes pass. I beep again. It's now 9.15.

Now bombs are going off in my head. I see what the real problem is in our house: I am not allowed to see my friend.

I beep a long time.

Liv appears. 'Wait a second,' she says.

Then she goes back into the house to fetch a biscuit for Cassady.

And then we go.

And finally at 9.30 a.m. we're outside Gary's house. I ring on his door several times. Eventually, the door opens. It's Lee, Gary's new boyfriend. He looks very handsome and slightly cruel.

'For God's sake,' he says, 'we were out till seven in the morning. It's a Saturday. We're not planning to get up till the afternoon.'

I go. I feel like I've tried to gatecrash a party, and I've been turned away at the door.

We slope off to the park. Luckily, it's a beautiful day, and the sun is shining through the leaves, and I start to cheer up. The kids run into the new playground. They both sprint to the climbing frame, and begin playing a game where they're pirates who are climbing the rigging.

Liv and I watch them. She's taken to wearing a turquoise colour, which matches her eyes. 'Sorry Gary wasn't up,' she says, putting a hand into my pocket. 'And thanks for getting them ready.'

''S OK,' I say. I'm accepting her apology but doing it in a wounded voice: I'm trying to show her she still owes me.

Liv squeezes my hand.

'Andrew,' she says, 'why don't we get married?'

I'm thinking: You devious bitch. You're only raising this now because you gatecrashed my date. Then I think: My goodness, this beautiful woman has just proposed marriage to me. I look at her.

'Erm . . .' I say. 'Cos weddings cost an average of twenty-five grand?'

'We'll do it cheap, and we'll do it quickly. Say, in four weeks' time.'

'But it'll still cost a lot, and they're not that much fun.'

'Why aren't they fun?'

'Cos weddings are supposed to be about love. But they're always about aunts, and vicars saying, "I shan't keep you long," and people whispering to each other, "I like your dress. Where did you get it?" And then the kids always cry during the vows, and then the mums pick them up, and they walk around in their designer clothes, being about as subtle as an erection in a sauna.'

'But the wedding wouldn't be about the kids,' she says. 'It'd be about us. We'll get a babysitter for the day.'

'Good,' I say, 'cos I hate bridesmaids upstaging the action. I don't want anyone looking cuter than me. Apart from you, of course.'

'Is that a yes?' she says.

'Of course! Although it seems a lot to arrange.'

'That's OK,' she says. 'I've already started.'

Suddenly I feel like I'm in a movie. In movies, as the hero has escaped the burning building, he always says to his lady: 'I love you. I could not live without you.' Audiences love hearing this line, because they don't hear it at home. I realize that it's true. I realize that Gary has forgotten our date, yet again, even though he suggested it. Livy is actually here. She is my date.

'Thank you, Livy,' I say. 'I'd be honoured to marry you.'

Livy and Grace

Rule 49: Be a gentleman: keep your friendships in good repair

September 2006, Dorset

I have to arrange my own stag weekend, though. I try to get Gary to do it, but he's off in the north of England shooting *Little Miss Jocelyn*. If I get to see him these days, I spend half the time hearing how busy he is. But mostly he texts to cancel. It's strange that I'm still trying to become successful; I loathe it when it happens to my friends.

I've been on loads of stag weekends, and have learned this: men love gathering without women. It's not really strippers that they want. They want to be able to make a mess without anyone telling them off. Stag weekends are always set in a rented country home, which the twenty stags decorate with beer cans and used socks. That's pretty much what I want, except I only want nine friends. I want a gentle, poetic sort of stag weekend. I want it to last three days. I want people taking walks, and laughing in the garden. And I don't like drinking. It's partly because I loathe all that macho 'get-it-down-ya' stuff. It's partly because I prefer smoking.

I assume it'll be no problem gathering the stags together. It is my stag weekend. That's the equivalent of a three-line whip. But I have only given two weeks' notice, and my friends have wives who don't want them to disappear for three days. They begin calling to say they *might* be able to make the Friday. Gary calls to ask if his boyfriend can come. I last saw that guy as he chased me away from Gary's house like I was a dog with rabies. I say there's no more space. Gary texts to say he can't make it at all.

I'm beginning to find this humiliating. I have got to the age of thirty-five, and I can't assemble nine friends. I can't even assemble my best man. Thankfully I'm one of four brothers. My family is like that Bob Hope joke: 'When we were kids, we all shared a bed together. If we said to Mum, "We're cold," she'd chuck another brother on.' Normally I love to criticize my brothers. Now I've never felt so thankful for them.

So the stags assemble. My brothers cook a dinner. After that I'm assuming we'll smoke bongs and have a laugh. But it's a Stag Weekend, and these things have an energy of their own. Within moments people are giving me cocaine, which is my least favourite drug. I can't get my head round a drug where the effects are always wearing off, so you're always sliding into disappointment. That's what life is like normally. I want to be brought *up*.

But it's hard to resist when someone else is paying. Before long I'm wasted and they're cracking open the tequila and everyone is hitting the table and shouting, 'Get it down ya!'

I spend the next day being violently sick, and most of the stags drift away.

By the last day, everyone has gone, except Nick Rowe. Nick knows exactly what I like to do. He agrees to get stoned. We lie on our backs giggling. Then we make up loads of stupid poems. We stand on a hillside, and we make up beautiful songs about Lou Gish. Once again, I see the fierce love he holds for her. I realize how lucky I am to love a woman who's still alive. Who's alive, and arranging the ceremony.

Now I'm ready to be married.

Rule 50: Find some angels

September 2006, Camden

We decide to get married in the church in Camden, right next to the zoo. We decide to invite no aunts, and no kids. I make a list, and I realize there are one hundred and twenty-six people that I really like. We decide we can only afford to have sixty guests, so I'll only be able to invite the people that I really, *really* like. I want to ask Patrick Malone to be the vicar. He's a friend of mine who's training for the priesthood.

He looks like Owen Wilson. He used to be an actor. Now he's training to be a vicar. I think he'll get more work that way. We once did a film together, and shared a caravan for three months. You go a bit mad if you spend that much time in a caravan with someone. We once had a fight. As part of a boyish jape, he rugby tackled me, really hurting my ankles. I chased after him, and then kicked him up the arse so hard that I damaged my foot.

I call up Patrick, and ask him to marry us.

'Why do you want *me*?' he says.

'Not many grooms could boast that they've had a fight with the vicar.'

'I've never done a marriage before,' he says. 'I'd be very nervous.'

'That's why I want you. Because you'd be saying the vows for the first time. Most vicars don't sound sincere. They sound like they're going through the motions.'

'I know what you mean,' says Patrick. 'But in marriages,

the burden of sincerity falls rather on the couple themselves. Do you want to do it?'

'Yes,' I say. 'Very much.'

'Great,' he says, 'then I'd love to do it for you.'

'OK,' I say. 'Well, let's talk about the crowd.'

'What do you mean?'

'I don't want them chatting to each other about their outfits.'

'What do you want?'

'High solemnity. The way I see it, those bastards have got an important job to do. We make the vows; they provide the glue by believing it's going to work. I don't want them talking about their holidays.'

'What do you want me to do? Shall I impose a prayer before it starts?'

'That would be perfect. How long can you stretch it?'

'A minute.'

'I want five.'

'Five minutes' silence?'

'Yep. That should do it. And then, once it starts, would you promise to give it *everything* you've got?'

Patrick laughs. 'I wish I'd never taken this gig.'

'Patrick, you'll be fine. But if you fool about I will step onto that altar and kick you up the arse.'

Three weeks later, we're outside the church in Camden. Inside, the crowd are taking their five minutes' silence. I just cast an eye over. If anyone talks, I'm going to get Patrick to throw them out. But Patrick is looking powerfully saintly, and it's commanding a certain reverence. Livy arrives. She's wearing a red dress, and a small headdress made out of gold leaves. She looks lovely. We're alone together. She grins and kisses me. As she does it, she breathes in slowly, like she wants to capture the moment. Then she does a low hum – 'hmmm' – like she wants to communicate a loving hum through my lips.

We prepare to go in. Liv didn't want to be given away by her dad. She loves him, but doesn't consider that she's his to give away. We're going in together. We hold hands. We walk down the aisle together, and everyone turns and smiles. I don't pay them too much mind. I don't want to distract them.

Patrick starts the show. He's hot with the Lord. He's possessed with Holy Fire. He kicks off with a hymn, and then he cracks straight into the vows. I'm staring into Liv's eyes, and I'm picturing all the things that Patrick is asking me to do. 'Will you love her? Will you keep her for so long as you both shall live?' Wow. That's a long time. How can I know? I glance at Liv. I glimpse the student I fell in love with and I can't believe I found her. 'I will,' I say.

Patrick builds the atmosphere further. He turns his Holy Eye on Livy. He's really working his magic now, striking a good bargain for me. She has to love me and keep me, in sickness and in health, forsaking all others – even if I'm sick, poor and boring, she has to stick around! And Patrick's selling it to her. I see no doubt in her eyes. 'I will,' she says.

Then the key moment comes. Patrick cranks it up like a Baptist preacher. He waves his arms, and he intones, in an incredible voice: 'I pronounce you *man* ... and **WIFE!!!**'

It's worked! I can feel that it's worked! Wow. I'm so proud of him, I give him a kiss. Then I realize we've just been pronounced man and wife, and I've just kissed the vicar.

And then my dad gets up to do a reading from Marcus Aurelius, and he prefaces it with a five-minute lecture on Roman mythology. I love it. And then Liv's dad plays a solo on his oboe.

At the end, we walk down the aisle, and as we walk between our sixty friends, every single one of them turns to us, and every single one of them smiles the most loving smile you've ever seen. Their love crashes towards us in a double wave.

And then we go off and have a reception. The comedian Phil Kay says grace, by improvising a song on a guitar. Gary makes a spectacularly misjudged speech, all about the time when we were on our way to interview Terry Gilliam, and I told him I'd just taken mushrooms. I love it, but the grans shift in their seats. I make a speech about Liv. I'm going after the Best Man speech. I've given myself top billing. Everyone laughs, and then they cry at the end. Then we put on our favourite music: 'Lone Star State of Mind', by Nanci Griffith; followed by Zorba the Greek; then Elvis, interspersed with the complete works of Louis Prima. Liv and I climb onto chairs, and we dance to Elvis's 'An American Trilogy'. Our friends are cheering us, as if we were Elvis. They want to give us more love. I want to say: 'It's OK. I don't need any more. I'm full.' But I don't. We just dance.

And then we fly to Siena for a five-day honeymoon in the Montepulciano hill country of northern Italy. Liv does let things down slightly by weeping and saying she misses the girls. I want to say: 'Surely I can be enough for you for five days! And by the way surely we're supposed to have sex at some point?' I don't say that. I say: 'You're very tired. Go to sleep.'

I have always wanted to go to Siena, since Gary told me that's the only place he's ever seen an angel. So naturally I'm desperate to see one. I leave the hotel early and I give Siena a quick recce. I don't even see the merest whiff of one. Not one halo. Not one wing kissed with golden light. Nothing. I'm standing in a coffee shop when I finally realize that

I'm disappointed. I need my wife to cheer up and get dirty. I need those bloody angels to stop skulking and make themselves visible. Those angels seem to be taking some kind of bank holiday. I need that to stop right now.

Livy arrives, smiling. 'Hi,' she says. 'I feel so much better.' I close my eyes while we kiss, and I smell the coffee. As I open my eyes, I notice that the walls of the coffee shop are covered with Ducio posters, which show angels with golden haloes. And I notice Livy is looking deliciously enticing. I see that I'm surrounded by angels. They're everywhere. You just have to know where to look.

This is an angel

She has a gold crown with two blue stars

You can't see her arms. They are tucked under her dress. I don't know what she does with her hands because I've never peeped under an angel's dress.

Rule 51: Teach them to be stupid

August 2006, Norfolk.
September 2006, Muswell Hill

This summer, Grace approaches some girls on the beach. 'Do you want to see a funny dance?' she says. They say nothing. She does Crazy Feet: that's the one where she kicks her feet manically, while pretending to fall over backwards. I love that dance. I cheer when she does it. But the Beach Girls turn away. They are four. They can already spot an idiot. I have a painful thought: I've taught her things that will hurt her.

This week is her first day at school. This is the mythical day that all parents wait for: the day when It Starts Getting Better. Before setting off, I ask her if she has any worries.

'Falling over in the playground,' she says. 'I don't want to hurt my knees.'

That is a worry. She's a very tall girl. All knees and elbows. She has more accidents than the average clown.

'Play next to the wooden train,' I say. 'There's a rubber floor.' She smiles. She knows I've banished all possible fears about education.

Finally it is time to go. 'I'm ready,' she says, and runs. The school is one hundred yards away. She makes it without hitting anything. In the playground, she sees Naomi, who she knows from playschool. She goes over. I sit nearby, feeling a bit proud, and a bit abandoned. She asks me over. Naomi is an old hand. Been at school three days already.

'What's fun about school?' I ask Naomi.

'You mix blue paint with bubble mixture,' she says. 'And you get a straw, and *blow into it*! And then you put paper over the bowl and it makes a pattern.'

'OK. But . . . is there *anything* to worry about?'

'*Yes!*' shouts Naomi. '*Sucking the straw!*'

We enter the classroom. Grace selects a white bridal dress from the dressing-up box. She asks me to help her into it. I feel this is the wrong decision. She's about to meet her class-mates for the first time. She might not want to be wearing a wedding dress. I help her into it.

For her first morning, I am allowed to stay. Dilemma: I don't want to interfere. But I don't want to hang about like an idiot.

So I do play dough. Merle shows me how to flatten. Lily gives me a cutter. Leo pushes play dough up my nose. I don't really mind. But I feel . . . I'm in school: there must be a rule about letting kids put play dough up your nose. I take it out, and say it smells of orange. I start a rumour that Mrs Popadopolis squeezes orange in the mixture. They all *scream* with laughter. I worry that, if I make another joke like that, I am going to get thrown out. But I am feeling good. I've made three friends already. Admittedly one of them put play dough up my nose.

I peek at Grace. She is quietly playing with water, wearing the bridal dress, looking like she's just heard her dog has died, but wants to be brave. I have a longing to take her away. I want to go back in time, and have her be one week old, so we can start all over again.

A boy comes up, slashing the air with a plastic knife. He looks vicious. He stops before her.

'What's your name?' she says.

'Alfie,' he says, in a surprisingly friendly voice. Silence.

'Alfie,' she says, 'do you want to see a funny dance?'

'OK.'

She launches into the Funky Chicken. Flapping wings. Jerky head. Everything. She looks like a daddy-long-legs being blasted by a hair dryer. I worry she could smack her elbows. She could maim someone. She could invite ridicule.

She stops. Alfie looks at her.

Then he laughs. I see she is going to be OK.

this is The Homework Can,
someone who can do the homework.

Rule 52: Do what Dahl says

October 2006, Great Missenden

Sunday. We're driving to the Roald Dahl Museum. I'm at the wheel, and in control. But Liv wants us to try 'the more scenic cut-through'. I object. I feel she is criticizing my routemanship, but she's persuasive. An hour later, the more scenic route has just led us into a field. In the back seat, the girls are having a violent argument.

Grace is growling menacingly: 'You are!'

Cassady is shouting: **'I'm not!'**

'You are!'

'I'm not! I AM NOT!'

'You are! You're *going* to die!'

Liv says: 'Andrew, tell Cassady she's not going to die.'

I say: 'Can you just tell me where I'm supposed to be bloody going?'

Luckily the girls' philosophical brains move to lighter mysteries.

'Daddy!' says Cassady. **'Where do babies come from?'**

'Ah,' says Grace, in her important voice. She feels she knows everything. She gets so many stickers from her teachers she comes home wearing a patchwork coat. I'm proud of her, but her education is making her painfully logical. Yesterday, she looked me in the eye and said outright: 'Daddy, fairies do *not* exist.' I'm with Spike Milligan on this: you always need to be in a house where someone believes in fairies.

'What happens,' explains Grace, 'is that Mummy and

Daddy have to get nude and then they sort of nudge together and then Daddy sort of wees and a sort of tadpole comes out.'

'*What?*' shouts Cassady, outraged. '**Then Daddy must NOT wee near me! I do NOT like babies!**'

'You love babies,' says Liv.

'**I hate them and I throw them out of windows.**'

We're back on the road now. I pass a building which is, I inform them, Boggis's farm, and I point out the very tree where Fantastic Mr Fox is even now hiding, and planning glorious mischief. They go silent. Roald Dahl's spell is working.

We get to the museum. It's a wonderful place that encapsulates Dahl's playful spirit. They spray the entrance with chocolate smell. They provide costumes for dressing up. They give you words you can use for making up Dahl sentences that get broadcast on the wall. An eight-year-old boy writes: 'The Stinking Giant Catapulted The Fat Mouse Into The Toilet.' I laugh. 'Very good,' I say.

'Rupert,' says his mother, 'wipe that off!'

They let you sit on Roald Dahl's actual chair, so you can make up stories. Liv makes for the chair. She sprawls on it wearing a Fantastic Mr Fox head. She makes up a story about a bumble bee that hurts its wing, so it goes to the waspital. Rupert's dad arrives as she finishes.

He looks around, disappointed. 'It's just a bloody chair,' he mumbles. I figure you can lead a horse to water, but you can't lead him to a waspital. Not unless you know the right route.

I sit in Dahl's chair. I close my eyes. 'Dahl!' I say. 'How do you get to a waspital?' I hear his voice in my head. It's warming, like the smell of Granny's cocoa.

'An excellent question,' he says. 'I'll answer with a poem.

Her herm. You must put a silly hat on./You must sit in my big chair./And if your wife gets naked,/Nudge together, and sniff her hair.'

On the way home, I suggest to Liv that we might nudge together one more time.

'I don't mind another baby,' she says, 'but I'm not sure I can face being pregnant. I can't carry another child. Can't you do it?'

Rule 53: Beware: your new skills will make you attractive

October 2006, Muswell Hill

Throughout my childhood, my dad waged a campaign against visitors. His strategy was to barricade them out with books, boxes and gloom. If visitors actually got into our house, he'd scowl from behind a paper.

I'm thinking about this now because suddenly we're being visited all the time. Other parents call up because they want their kids to play with ours. They always lounge around saying, 'Don't you think parents are competitive about their children?' And I always want to say: 'I'm not competitive about your children. I'm not remotely interested in them. I have to screen them out, or I'd never have a social life.' But I don't say that, because I'm not insane.

We're also getting loads of single visitors, who come if they've just been chucked, or if they've just met someone and want to know if they should call. They drink wine and tell me about the different kinds of crap men ... Men who are scared of commitment. Men who should be committed to mental hospitals. Men who wear gel on the front of their hair so it looks like they've plunged their heads into lard. For the first time in years, I'm in danger of becoming popular. I think it's because I've learned to listen. I've spent all my life trying to be witty. I now know people hate that. They want you to treat them like children. They want you to say: 'What?' and 'What happened next?' and 'You poor thing ... Now, let me cook you scrambled eggs.'

It's OK. But it's all a bit tame. That's why lately I've been dying to see my friend Sedley. You remember in *It's A Wonderful Life* where Jimmy Stewart is just about to travel the world and have adventures, when he makes the mistake of falling in love and having a family. Sedley is the guy who got away. He spent a year in the mountains of Peru, hanging out with terrorists and writing poems. Then he went to New York where he played in a band. Then he went to the Maldives where he started his own scuba-diving school. But he always says the best fun he ever had was when we were at college and we shared a flat together.

So you can imagine how excited I am when he calls up to say he's leaving the Maldives. He wants to come and stay. I'm in boy heaven. The first night we stay in and watch four episodes of *24*. I love *24*. In an average hour, Jack Bauer kills three villains, foils a nuclear plot, and beats the crap out of his brother – something we all long to do once in a while. In an average day, I can't even find a babysitter. If I get two refusals, I give up. I hide under the duvet and groan.

The next night Sedley and I go clubbing. I dance, but then I catch myself jiving like a dad at a wedding. A girl comes on to me a bit so I feel guilty and go outside and call home. Eventually, I find myself outside the toilet, trying to talk to a bloke called Mike. He shouts to me: 'So where do you live?' I yell back: 'Muswell Hill.' He shouts: 'What?' I shout: 'Muswell Hill.' He shouts: 'What?' I scream: '*Muswell Hill!*' and I suddenly boil over with self-hatred.

I find Sedley and tell him I need to go home. He shouts in my ear: 'I've just got some Es. Don't you want one?' I shout back: 'No!' He shouts back: 'Don't you like Es?' And I want to shout: 'I've got nothing against them. I've got nothing against dancing. I just think they should be done in the day-time. It's three in the morning, for God's sake!' But I don't say that. It's awful hanging out with someone who's being rock 'n' roll and rebellious. It forces you to be the sensible one.

The next day, I'm too tired to work or do childcare. Which is just as well, since I need to tidy. The sofa has been redesigned by Tracey Emin. It's surrounded by used socks, men's magazines and dried up bowls of cereal. I clear it all up, and I realize something weird has happened. I've become a parent; now people think I'm their parent. When I come in, Sedley is in the living room, air-guitaring to Jeff Buckley. He's also smoking.

'Sedley! Did you have a good time last night?'

'Amazing. Unreal. How are you? How's work?'

I say to him: 'For God's sake! I haven't done any work, because I've been looking after you. It's fine if you want to sleep on sofas, but I'm the one clearing up your cereal bowls. Now will you get out of my house, you stupid childish waste of space!'

Of course I don't say that. I'm polite. I grab a newspaper. I sit down. And I scowl.

It works though. Because soon after, Sedley leaves and the sun comes out, so the girls and I go outside and get into the paddling pool.

Grace says:

'Right! How many toes are in this paddling pool?'

Now that's a question I can answer. We start counting toes happily. I don't need friends. I've bred two companions who are perfect.

My dad greets his guests

Rule 54: Give love, but don't expect it in return. (Generosity is its own reward, especially if you're giving out syphilis)

December 2006, Muswell Hill

I've got this granny who's ninety-one, but nothing can kill her. Till seven years ago, she was still doing a meals-on-wheels round. One day, she wrenched her arm out of the socket. She finished her rounds, and then drove herself to hospital. If there were a nuclear blast, my gran would emerge from the rubble holding an ugly jumper she'd just knitted. She'd look around at the ruined buildings. She'd offer her standard opinion: 'It's a shame!'

Ten years ago, she came on holiday with us to Cornwall. She brought two surfboards with her. Well, she called them surfboards. Really they were just planks of wood, which she had lying around in the shed. 'Nana,' I said to her, 'I think your surfing days are over.' But she was determined to go. The next day she set off down the beach with one of her surfboards under her arm. She was wearing a floral swimsuit and a rubber swim hat. Surfers don't normally wear that. They also, generally, don't have wonky knees and plastic hips. Worried, but somewhat impressed, I watched her walk towards the horizon. She was blasted sideways by the howling wind. She waded into the sea and hurled herself into the path of the biggest breaker she could find. Then she disappeared. Her limbs couldn't take the water. She was like a wet spider going down the plughole. I sprinted over. By the time I reached her, she was breathing between waves.

For some reason, I'm thinking about this as I turn my phone on.

I see I've got a text. It says: 'Nana died ten minutes ago. Mum.' It was left ninety minutes ago. Livy rings. I tell her.

She says: 'So Val's at home with the girls?'

'Yes.'

'What are you doing?'

'Driving to Gary's.'

'Why are you still driving to Gary's?'

Good question. Cos he's my friend and I take every chance to see him. Cos an obnoxious guest left a bag of weed at his party. Gary's offered it to me.

'I need to pick up some work,' I say.

'You should be comforting your mum,' says Liv. 'You're so selfish.'

I nearly say: 'So are you. You're just worried about the girls.' But I don't. In marriage, attack is never the best form of defence.

Gary opens the door. We hug. I skin up. I say: 'My gran's just died.'

He says: 'Were you close?'

'No one was close to her. Not even my mum, and she visited her once a week. She said Nana never loved her, she just criticized her. And was so old most of her organs started life inside someone else. She's been trying to die for the last six years.'

'She needed to go,' he says, and bursts into tears. Gary experienced his own loss two weeks ago: his dog died. The Irish water spaniel. He got a brain tumour and passed away suddenly. Gary's been crying for a week now. We all participated in a fantastic funeral for the dog. We went to Hampstead Heath, bearing a biodegradable urn of doggie ashes. We sang songs and danced. Gary fell to his knees like a caveman, and he tore at the earth with his bare hands, and he buried his dog under a gigantic pine. It was a magnificent occasion. I can't wait for his next dog to die. I want to do it all again.

I hug my friend. I tell him I don't want to go home cos my mum'll be crying, and I'll have to hug her.

'I know,' he says. 'But you will.'

When I get home I go straight up to the kids' room. My mum is doing stories. I've rarely seen her so cheerful. I read stories, then kiss the girls goodnight and get downstairs just in time for the Big Moment: Mum is dialling her brother Graham. A twice-divorced accountant who was the apple of Nana's eye. The word is she left him everything.

'Mother's gone,' says Mum. Then: 'The hospital are only interested in the corneas.' *Her mother's just died!* Already, we're discussing the recycling of the body. OK, Nana hated waste, but this seems astonishing. Mum continues: 'I'm selling the house straight away ...' I'm wondering how Graham's taking this. I lean into the phone. He's saying: 'You don't think the kitchen would prejudice a buyer?'

I go outside. I smoke the weed. I shut my eyes, and I say, 'Nana,' and I see her. She's got bruised eyes, but she looks pleased. I say: 'I loved visiting you when we were small. Grandboy would be teasing. You'd be turned away making cocoa.'

'Well,' says the Nana in my mind, 'I was letting him talk. He was being funny.' And I suddenly cry. 'Thank you,' I say, and I kiss her crinkly white hair. 'Goodbye.'

I go back in and I give my mum a hug, which confuses her, and a glass of wine, which she understands perfectly. 'To Nana,' I say. 'Congratulations on a successful escape!' We clink glasses.

My mum is a giggler. On a good day, I can get her to fall

from her chair, and roll about on the floor. 'Well,' I say, 'Philip Larkin said: "What shall survive of us is love." If he'd met Nana, he may have said: "What shall survive of us is a bungalow filled with cat food. And some corneas no one wants."'

My mum laughs, but she doesn't fall off her chair.

The last time Nana went surfing

Rule 55: Become a man

December 2006, Norfolk and Muswell Hill

I wake. I check my phone: 7.20 a.m. I slept for six hours, forty-two minutes. I see a sign saying: BREAKFAST IS 'SERVED' BETWEEN 7–9 A.M.. I wonder: why is 'served' in inverted commas? Is breakfast distributed through a pipe? I piece together what's happening. I'm in a cheap B&B in Norfolk. Last night I did a show: two hours of new material. It went well. These days I pretend that the audience are children, and they prefer that.

My phone rings. An angry voice says:

'It's Robin *Dingley* here.' I have no idea who Robin Dingley is. 'There are *scaffolders* outside your house.'

'Great,' I say. I figure Robin Dingley is the Site Manager for our loft conversion job, which starts tomorrow.

'They've arrived at seven o'clock on a Sunday morning! That's not *great!*' says Robin Dingley, who's clearly furious. I realize it's my neighbour: Robin. As in Robin and Sue. I visited them, yesterday, to assure them that we would be doing ANYTHING to make the building work as quiet as possible. Less than twenty-four hours later, he's been woken by the sound of some ruffian youth shouting: 'Chuck me the spanner, you dozy cunt.'

I assure Robin Dingley I'm in control of the situation. I turn my phone off and go to breakfast. I sip coffee and read about England's nil-all draw against Israel. Why is Steve McClaren managing England? I *said* that Martin O'Neill was the only choice for the job. I said this would happen.

Obviously I said it to my wife. Sadly, she lacks contacts within the FA, and doesn't know, or care, who Martin O'Neill is. I have explained to her who Martin O'Neill is, but I could see that glazed look in her eye. She was mentally shelving Martin O'Neill into a big file named Things I Don't Need To Think About.

When I turn the phone on Robin Dingley has called another three times. He informs me: 'I've phoned the council, and it's actually illegal to have work done on a Sunday.' I live in suburbia. We don't curse, we exchange very firm messages, in which we hint at legal procedures. I try to phone Liv, but she's at her mum's. Liv's phone is off. The home phone isn't working.

I drive back to London.

I open the front door. Liv arrives. 'Hi!' she says. 'Did the gig go OK?'

'Yes.'

'Right. You need to empty the attic NOW. I'll help.'

'Can I just eat?'

'We need to get it done by five. Val's arriving for tea.'

I go upstairs and open the trapdoor to the attic. A rickety ladder squeak squeak squeaks down. We go up. The attic is packed full of stuff. We take either end of some curtain poles, and lift. Well ... I lift. Liv goes: 'Ooh, hang on a second ... oh ... Just wait ... Put it down.' I see what she's doing. She sees me as the manager of the attic-emptying project; she's trying to demonstrate she's an unwilling employee who should be sacked.

'Just ... let me do this,' I say gruffly. I take over.

Two hours later, I've done about three quarters of it. I'm dusty. I'm sweaty. Testosterone is surging round my system. I'm feeling angry, and unusually manly. I bring down ten unopened IKEA shelves that, a year ago, I told her we'd definitely never want again. I bring down the pissy child's mattress that should've been thrown out. Yes, OK, shut up … I'm also bringing down my videos I swore I would sort out last summer. I hate everything in the attic. When an object goes into storage, it's like a person going to Death Row. Occasionally something gets a reprieve; most items are never seen again. I hate the attic. It reminds me of my parents' house, which I can't bear. My parents have corridors that are double-lined with books. They have rooms with doors that you can't open, because they're blocked by piles made out of old furniture, *Sunday Times* newspapers from the year 1993 and maternity bras that belonged to my grandmother. My dad is always smoking Silk Cut, which fill the air with a cloying chemical smell. And my mum is always manically brandishing a red-hot tray of cooking while saying things like: 'Oh-I-didn't-expect-you-so-soon-WHY-didn't-you-come-the-Birmingham-route-now-DO-COME-IN-I've-got-you-some-natural-yoghurt!'

I'm coming down the rickety stepladder, bearing some curtains that we've NEVER used and I've always hated. It would be hard for the situation to become more annoying than it is. I can hear the TV playing the horrible *Big Cook, Little Cook* jingle where they sing tunelessly about having the cleanest kitchen in town. I hate that song. I want to visit their superclean kitchen, and fill it with cement. The dog has arrived. She's stalking me, trying to get me to feed her. At that moment, my box splits open, and the contents gush out.

I swear, quite colourfully. Livy hears. Swearing is the one thing she won't allow. To her it's worse than adultery. In fact, she'd probably forgive me adultery, provided I didn't describe it afterwards.

She says: 'Will you stop having tantrums?'

I get to the bottom of the stepladder, but my path is blocked by moist cardboard. I kick it quite forcefully out of the way. Now I'm not saying I'm behaving in a dignified manner at this point. But there's a difference between kicking a box AT someone, and kicking a box into an empty room when you're trying to get it out of the bloody way.

'You're just like your dad,' she says. That's harsh. I'm not *just* like my dad; I'm a bit like my dad. And anyway he has golden qualities. They're hidden behind a fug of fag smoke and rage, but they're there. I am sorely tempted to shout: 'When I'm angry will you just leave me alone! I'm the one who's moving the bloody boxes!'

I say nothing. I delete Livy from my mental computer screen. I pick up the IKEA shelves and carry them to the front of the house.

The girls are out on the pavement, having some kind of running race.

'**Daddy!**' says Cassady. '**She is not letting me win!**'

Grace is saying: 'But it's a RACE, Daddy. Tell her.'

The girls both look at me. I see I've drifted into a little courtroom situation. I am the judge.

'Tell her, Daddy,' says Grace again. 'It's a race so she can't make me try and lose!'

Cassady looks suspicious. She can see the case is drifting away from her. She's no match for her sister's silky rhetorical skills. She screams.

At this point Grace notices that I've chucked out her blue plastic keyboard. The one my mum bought in Woolworths for £34.99. The one with the yellow plastic button that Cassady keeps pressing, so we always hear the same four notes. The girls love that keyboard.

'Why is this here?' says Grace. I have a horrifying realization. I see that the hoarder gene misses a generation.

238

My parents are both hoarders: so I crave minimalism: my girls are hoarders.

'I don't know why that is here,' I say, and carefully lift the keyboard down.

Liv comes out of the house. She can see that Cassady is still screaming. I appear to be doing nothing about it. It's imperative that I solve this situation before she reaches us.

'Cassady,' I say, in my firmest voice. 'Be calm. You must stop shouting. Hold my hand. We're going inside.'

Cassady instantly goes quiet. Liv sees I've solved the situation.

She says: 'I've made you some tea. Why don't you come in?'

Something strange has happened. She senses my new manliness, and has responded by going all womanly.

'I've got some flowers,' she says, 'for next door.'

'Good,' I say. She looks very lovely, and her eyes are very blue. I want to say something like: 'Well done, My Queen.' But if I say that, she'll reckon I'm stoned. And I'm actually not. I haven't done that in weeks.

We've all reached the front door when a blue Saab turns up. It's my mum. She gets out. Her dog runs for our front door. My dog intercepts her, and beats the crap out of her.

'Hello, Mum,' I say.

'What are you all doing outside?' she says. 'Now you can GIVE THIS BACK if you don't want it . . .' She is tugging something out of the boot of her car. It appears to be some plastic garden furniture. 'It's a TABLE!' she says. 'If you don't want it, just say now.'

I look at my mum. I want to take that plastic piece of garden furniture. I want to chuck it clean over the neighbours' house. I want to shout at my mum. It bugs me that she's still not said hello and kissed me. Now stop. Don't even start suggesting there's something Freudian going on here. I really don't want my mum to get sexy with me. I just want her to say hello. And I want her to stop bringing us stupid plastic objects.

'Hello, Mum,' I say, kissing her. She turns at the last moment, and gets me on the lips. I can feel the moisture. 'It's a very kind thought,' I say, 'but I'm going to say no to the table.'

'Fine,' she says. She turns away. She's deeply wounded that I've rejected her present. She hugs and kisses both girls, and then she pulls some plastic bags out of the back seat. 'I've brought you both something,' she says, and gives each girl a plastic bag. For Grace she's brought a book of Babar stories. For Cassady she's brought a fairy castle, which you can assemble out of wooden pieces. Both gifts are perfect. The girls are so excited they can hardly speak.

I leave them inspecting their presents. I go upstairs. I check the attic. I fling down the last couple of bags. I find a box of stories I wrote when I was eight. The first one is called Jack The Brave Police Dog. Jack was everything I wanted to be when I was eight. He was a detective. He worked for the police. He was a dog. His catchphrase was: 'Ho-hum, what's all this then? Woof!' I'm glad we kept that.

Liv arrives. 'I've run you a bath,' she says. I see what she's saying. I see how she wants me to respond. 'Thanks,' I say, and I kiss her, quite forcefully, on the lips. I go upstairs. I see the bath is indeed run. For the last time, I close up the annoying squeaky trapdoor. I see that the job is done. I get into the bath.

Rule 56: Leave your kids alone.
Just watch them

December 2006, Muswell Hill

I'm just not Christian. I know some people go to church, but it's noticeable that they all live outside the catchment area for the decent schools. But my girls are more open-minded. They love Jesus. They prefer Snow White, but they love Jesus. Jesus has donkeys; Snow White has dwarves.

Six p.m. I'm working. Cass arrives. She says: '**Do you want to read my book OK you can.**' She presents me with a notebook filled with writing and three-year-old art: smiley people with arms growing out of their heads. '**That's a angel**,' she says, '**what says to Mary you're going to have a baby what's called Babyjeezus.**' (To be quite accurate, the text reads: 'HoK FleF Menerm G'.)

She turns over. '**And the angel's mummy says: "Go to Bethlehem to be counted."**' She turns over. '**The soldier counts them: "One, two, three …"**' I always panic when kids start counting. You never know how long it'll last. Luckily, at fourteen, she gets stuck. Fourteen is as high as she can go. At that height, she runs out of oxygen. She says: '**Fourteen, fourteen RIGHT, there's TWENTY people in Bethlehem.**'

Grace arrives. She sees herself as the theological expert, since she's in a nativity play playing a reindeer. We've been rehearsing for weeks. If any of those reindeer fall ill, I'll be straight in there. It'll be my first acting job in months.

'At Bethlehem,' says Grace, 'there's NO ROOM at the inn.' Kids always remember this bit: the accommodation details. The implication is that, while Babyjeezus is laying down his sweet head in the manger, everyone else is in a Trust House Forte, where they've got tea, shortbread and a Corby trouser press.

I send everyone to bed. Tomorrow morning is show time.

My mistake is taking drugs beforehand. I have one of those awful nights where I wake at 3 a.m., and I take one Nytol an hour till I finally crash at seven. Livy wakes me at 9.30. The show starts in ten minutes.

We have to run for it.

The headmistress welcomes us. 'Everyone must stay seated,' she says. 'Otherwise the children notice you, and start crying.' Sixty parents nod obediently.

Reassured, the headmistress lets the kids in. There's a screeching of chairs as twenty dads scramble to their feet, training cameras at the arriving procession of sheep, angels and reindeer. It's like seeing Wayne Rooney going through on goal. It's too exciting. We can't stay seated. To make it worse, the mums start waving, and the reindeers, showing no respect for the Fourth Wall, wave back. And then I notice teachers hidden amongst the cast. Their job is to lead the singing – like those blokes at football matches who spend the whole game shouting: 'Come on ... Sing! ... *We are Arsene Wenger's army ...*'

Only now do I see Grace. During the night, she's developed a shocking bout of conjunctivitis. The other reindeer are ushering her. She's holding a tissue over her eye. Tears stream down her cheeks. She's highly professional though. Sobbing, she sings all the words we've rehearsed. She does all the actions. She hits her cue and says her line.

Yes, her eyes are shut, like Chris Martin singing a sad bit, but she's nice and loud.

But then she loses her tissue. She weeps inconsolably, but silently.

Nativity plays are painful experiences anyway. It's like seeing your kids through the playschool window: you can see them; you can't touch them. It makes you extra aware of the love you feel for them. But this tragic sight is particularly moving. She looks so small and helpless and I feel so much love for her it hurts. So I suppose, in its way, it's all rather Christian.

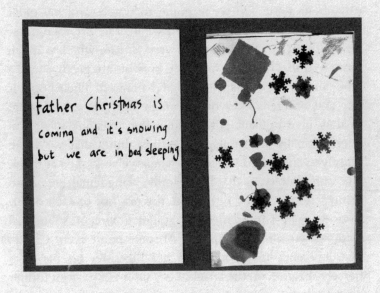

Father Christmas is coming and it's snowing but we are in bed sleeping

Rule 57: Don't be prissy.
Just hang out with your family

Christmas 2006, a small village
near Plymouth

For British couples, the most divisive subject is money. For us, it's Christmas. For the last three years we've gone to her family. My family is very male. It's full of vast men who like staying up till 4 a.m., while they eat and make a mess and take the piss out of each other. At some point, we'll have a row about what TV we're going to watch, and my older brother will punch me, and then we'll all ignore each other for another year. Liv's family is very female, which is much more restful. The neatly wrapped presents are given one at a time, and each gift is applauded and admired. Their house is tidy and ordered. Everyone is much better at empathizing, so they give brilliant gifts because they imagine what you might like. In my family, we all buy things that we'd like ourselves, and we pass them on when we've looked at them. The only problem is that Liv's family, being female, are all so damn sensitive. They never take the piss out of each other. Instead, each family member wages a violent subtextual battle to win all the sympathy. At some point every Christmas, Liv ends up crying, and her big sister resents it so fiercely she goes on the attack. Liv's sister is a six-foot former model who now runs a publicity department in a big publishing house. She's magnificent and fiery, like an avenging queen. This year, she's had twins. I daren't go within fifty miles of her.

This year, Liv starts the bargaining early. We'll spend the Christmas week with her family, she proposes, and we'll 'maybe try' to see my family in the autumn. I say we should split up for Christmas, or indefinitely, if necessary; I would be going home. 'It might be my Big Dad's last Christmas,' I say, almost weeping. 'You say that every year,' she says. 'Big Dad will still be around in ten years. We'll be seeing him for Christmas. He'll still be acting like an ox that's sat on a wasp.'

Then my mum announces she and Big Dad have rented a large holiday home: they hope we can all join them. I feel that clinches it. We're joining them.

Everyone moves on to the matter of presents. My little brother suggests a big pampering scheme for Mum; other brothers chip in. I say Mum doesn't like pampering; she's of that generation that feels embarrassed about having their feet looked at. She likes theatre. I say I'm getting eleven tickets for *Spamalot*; I hope they can all come. My big brother sends me two pages of abuse: 'Oh … you hate our idea … you'll only listen to someone else provided they're gay/your new best friend/or someone who's on television.' In a family, the eldest sibling is the angry Heir Apparent. They don't like anything to happen unless they're in charge.

I'm about to email back when I get a sad, cold feeling inside. I realize my brother hates me. Then I realize they all do. But I reckon that, if I email everyone a very meek apology, then it'll swing the balance of sympathy back to me.

Luckily my big brother writes to say he's spending Christmas with just his own wife and kids. They're going to Cuba. That makes it a bit easier, but I'm still looking forward to Christmas the way a tramp looks forward to his annual blast of the disinfectant spray. I'm expecting a blast of cold criticism, which, I've learned, will ultimately be good for me.

Eventually, 23 December comes round. I drive the whole family to Plymouth. I run out of petrol half a mile from the holiday home. My little brother rescues me. He's fairly gracious, but he huffs a lot. He wants me to know he's doing me a favour, and I owe him.

We get to the holiday home. It's a disaster. It's eight draughty bedrooms, arranged around two avocado bathrooms. Outside the tiny kitchen, there's a windowless toilet, which already stinks of bleach. Inside the kitchen, the chairs screech noisily against a stone floor, and there's an Aga that's scalding hot and pumping out heat. You don't need to be Laurence Llewellyn-Bowen to predict that this kitchen is a weak spot.

It turns out there's a further problem. This Christmas week is the highlight of my mum's year; she's responded by going insane. She's absurdly tense. It's like she's mainlining coffee. She's heard about the email argument. She's mortified it happened on her behalf. Now she's determined not to show me any favouritism, since everyone knows she does childcare for us, and they all think I don't pay her enough.

My mum is allocating the kids bunk beds, which are next to the TV room. She gives me and Liv a tiny room, which can only be approached through Chris's bedroom. Chris is my youngest brother. He won't even arrive for another day, and he's a DJ. His favourite leisure activity is smoking to late-night TV. Liv reckons my brother should sleep next to the TV; us four should have the adjoining rooms. She wants me to tell everyone, but insists I make out it's my idea.

In the kitchen, I propose the new bedroom arrangement. My mum has a kind of catatonic fit.

She says: 'Well, you'll have to speak to Chris.'

Christmas Eve. Chris arrives. I hug him, and then ask straight away. I tell him Liv is pregnant. We've not told anyone till now. We've not needed to. I tell him I'll do him anything in return. I go to bed.

Christmas morning. The kids wake at 6 a.m. I occupy them for three hours, but then Liv starts crying. It's the season. She can't help it. She has a headache, but isn't allowed drugs. I put a video on, and attend. Now my brother is woken.

He's furious.

Within moments the family is gathering in the tiny kitchen like a herd of bad-tempered bison. 'You did say you'd do anything,' says the brother who always takes the moral high ground. I say sorry. I feel terrible.

I go upstairs, and speak to Liv. She says: 'Let's leave first thing Boxing Day.' That is the traditional time of Christmas walk-outs. Boxing Day always wakes to the sound of revving engines.

And then I take the girls for a long walk. My sister comes with us, because she wants to go skinny-dipping. We reach the sea. Cassady sees a rock pool, which, she declares, is the very place from which The Little Mermaid first glimpsed her Handsome Prince. I get to play the prince. Then my sister strips and runs in the sea. She's shy at the moment, because she thinks she's two stone overweight. She's been living in Scotland, where she's been relishing the national diet of beer and chips. As she jumps in the sea, her bottom is fleshy and pink. She's a Beryl Cook painting, come to life. We all cheer my sister's bottom, which is the most pleasing thing I've seen in ages.

Then my sister dresses, and takes Grace and Cass by the hand. They walk home. I walk home alone. I think of my eighth Christmas when my big brother said I was a Jumbo ·

Jet End – a reference to the shape of my willy, which I found profoundly upsetting, although I didn't really understand it. I retreated to the wasteland, and made a fortress. My brother made one nearby. It became more of a siege, than a war. We spent a long time rearranging our defences, and occasionally shouting abuse. Then my mum said it was time for lunch and we came home. That's the reality of family warfare: you spend a lot of time rearranging your defences, but the attacks are never quite as bad as you expect.

At home, I tell Chris we're thinking of leaving in the morning since it's hard being the only parents in a house of adults. He says he doesn't like being woken up, but, if I leave, he'll be furious. We hug. Then we go outside and smoke something that my mum refers to as A Big Christmas Squiffie. Sadly, my mum won't have any. Then Chris and I discover a table-tennis table in the garage. We start to play. By lunchtime I'm 8–6 up.

Then we go in to eat, and the kids are all proud to be sitting round the big table. My little brother puts a tape on: the John Lennon Christmas song, the one where Yoko Ono screeches like a cat being burned. If music is the food of love, Ono is the anchovy. My dad says: 'I don't mind if you want to listen to this shit. I'll just go and eat in the kitchen!' We laugh. We turn it off. We toast the cook. We eat the lunch.

And then afterwards we open the presents. My mum goes mental about gifts. She favours the cheap-and-cheerful items, especially if they're in the sale. She's given everyone a sackful of stuff, which all feature stickers saying 50% OFF. She's wrapped up boxer shorts, and shaving cream, and packets of spaghetti. She's given my kids a whole bin bag each, crammed with gifts. There's nothing of the tasteful restraint of Livy's family. Before long, the living room is

248

strewn with paper and cheap plastic items. My mum is drinking a triple gin and tonic. Even my dad is smiling. We're all having a fantastic time.

From left to right: me smiling serenely while shoving my little brother out of shot; James, my little brother who's twenty-three months younger than me – he's now a surgeon; I've no idea who that curly haired child is, but I hope he's recovered from my brother grabbing his crotch; my big brother, now a merchant banker.

Rule 58: Understand that your life is a fairy story

February 2007, Muswell Hill

I hate it when people say: 'The wedding was lovely. It was like a fairy tale!' People know *nothing* about fairy tales. Fairy tales don't involve fake tan and Bollinger and people in Gucci taking coke in the toilets.

If you read enough fairy tales, you realize you're in one, because they are metaphors for the way life actually feels. Fairy tales always start in chaos: *The Queen is dead. The King's remarried. The world is wrong.* That's how we all feel. George Bush rules, while Al Gore is sidelined. And we're sidelined ourselves. We should be royalty. We're not. We're cleaning floors while Ugly Sisters rule. We've all got our own Ugly Sisters. Mine are Jimmy Carr, and Graham Norton, and anyone else who's earning six million a year, while I'm sponging off Liv.

I don't have a wicked stepmother. I just have a wife. Yes, she's not wicked, but I'm programmed to feel that she is. Because I know that, in a fairy tale, the story doesn't begin until the witch attacks.

Over breakfast, it happens.

Liv says: 'I forgot to tell you. Your agent called yesterday. You've got an audition.'

'Not another one!' A fortnight ago I went up for an American mini-series called *Sadie the Wolverine*, a sort of *Buffy* rip-off, in which I'd play a kind of rip-off of the Anthony Head character. A typical line was: 'You're certainly developing your powers.' I couldn't say it without making it sound dirty. I felt like a Latin teacher with an erection. I have no confidence for auditions. I always want to say: 'I know you really want Ewan McGregor. Just to make it easier for you, I've not learned my lines.'

'This is just an advert casting this morning,' says Liv. 'You've got to be a dancing pirate.'

'I never get adverts,' I say, 'because I can't smile when I feel uneasy. I need to write today.'

'What are you writing?'

'Eighth draft of *Dirty Angels*.'

'Why are you redrafting it?'

'I want to make it so that people's eyes are stapled to the page.'

'Look. You have to make an effort. Go and do the advert casting. Who knows what could happen? It could earn us money!'

'So could my novel. And I'd rather spend the day writing.'

'For God's sake!'

'Do you not believe,' I say grandly, 'I can earn money from writing?'

'*No, I don't!*' she says, suddenly snapping, and I panic. My own wife doesn't believe in me. Worse, she's attacking the thing I love most: writing. In that moment, I'm Snow White. She's the wicked stepmother telling a hunter to cut out my heart. I feel the rush of wind, as he jabs towards my chest.

In fairy stories, the heroine runs off to the forest, where she finds dwarves or fairies or talking mice. I go into the garden and light a fag. That's when the fairy arrives. It's Grace.

She says: 'Why are you smoking?'

'I'm cross.'

'Why?'

'Because Mummy's making me go into town, where I have to pretend to be a pirate.'

She studies me. She says: 'You could make a pirate moustache.'

I kiss her. I see how bristly I am. I've not shaved in a week. I go in. I shave, leaving a moustache and pointed mini beard. I look like a thick pirate who once went to school with Francis Drake. Suddenly I want to do the casting.

But getting there is impossible. I get as far as Grace's school when my bike collapses. I'm flung over the wheel. I somersault on the pavement, and look back. The mudguard has got caught in the front wheel. I know what I must do: I must stomp that bike till it's mangled. I'm about to start, when I see I've got an audience. Whenever I pass Grace's school, the kids line up along the fence shouting, 'Hello, Grace's daddy!' and we all have a laugh. They think I was doing a stunt for them. The boys want me to do it again.

Grace has seen the problem.

'Did you hurt yourself?' she says.

'I'm OK. But the bike is ruined, and I have to go into town.'

'You're going to have to go on the train.'

'I know. Thanks, honey.'

I go home and chuck the bike over the wall. I walk the twelve minutes to the tube. The ticket office says: 'Your card's been refused.' The card looks how I feel: scratched; the signature's worn off. I hurry home. I find the card from my old account. I run back. I'm now late and tense. A woman is standing by the ticket office, sorting through her bag. I shove my card under the window. 'One travelcard please.'

The woman says: 'Don't you fucking queue?'

I look up, and see a wicked witch wearing a Nicole Farhi coat.

'Sorry,' I stutter. 'Thought you'd finished.'

'Don't stand there,' she says, glaring. 'Stand behind me.'

I stand behind her. I feel shaky. My heart is beating. I smell the scalded cauldron.

Eventually, she goes. I hand the old card to the ticket man. He tells me to punch in my pin. I do, but I'm not confident I remember it, or that there's any money in the account.

He says: 'That's been approved.' And I hear the tinkling of a fairy godmother sprinkling fairy dust. 'Great,' I say to the ticket man, 'now I must hurry to the ball.'

'You're going to a ball?' he says.

'Well,' I say, 'an advert casting.'

On the tube, I'm still thinking about fairy tales. I know that Cinderella does make it to the ball, although she does it in borrowed robes in a carriage made from a pumpkin. I stop off in Soho Square, and smoke a pipe. Now I'll be able to smile.

In the reception of the casting, I see four other pirates. They're all twenty-five. I fill in a form. I say I'm twenty-eight. I'm thirty-six.

Then I'm shown into the ballroom itself – the casting suite. Prince Charming, the director, is eating a crabstick sandwich. He says: 'Could you take your top off?' As I strip, I notice tufty hair on my shoulders. They roll the cameras. They play music. I dance like a desperate man needing cash.

For ten seconds.

'Thank you,' he says.

'Thank *you*,' I say.

While I dress, Prince Charming talks to the cameraman about *Little Britain*.

On leaving, I have a thought that's never appeared in any fairy tales: If I walk another step, my blisters will burst like grapes. I text Liv, and ask her to pick me up from the station. Then I remember she's gone out.

As I leave the tube station, it's raining. I rummage for a cagoule in my bag. A hand touches my shoulder. It's Livy.

'Your agent called,' she says. 'They want you for *Sadie the Wolverine*. He says you'll earn at least three grand a week. They want you to fly to Canada to meet everyone.'

'Oh ... good,' I say. I'm always bashful about receiving good news. I don't want to look like I'm boasting, or I feel someone will attack me.

'Well done,' she says. 'I'm very proud of you.'

She kisses me on the lips, and I'm woken from a hundred-year sleep.

'The only trouble is,' she says, 'you'll have to move to Vancouver for two years.'

'OK. Let's talk about that,' I say. 'Where are the fairies?'

'What are you talking about?'

'The girls.'

'They're in the car.'

Just then I see them. They're sticking princess stickers on the windows. They see me. They both shout and wave. I get into the car. Liv says: 'Right, girls. What are we going to say?'

'Hurray for Dad!' they both say. Except Cass says, '**Ray for Dad!**' which sounds like she's telling me about a man called Ray who's got a crush on me.

Then we go home.

I can't say we live happily ever after. But we have eggs for tea.

A Witch pretending
to be a Mummy. Her
bat has turned
into a pink bag.

Rule 59: Turn up

March 2007, Muswell Hill

I'm in the garage smoking. Liv arrives. 'You're supposed to be reading stories for Grace's class!' she says. 'You've got to be there in five minutes!' My stomach jumps, like I've just been hurled out of a plane. I run upstairs, and search for books. I know what I want to read: the illustrated book I made a few months ago.

It was called *The Princess Fairy*. It's all about this bear who lands in fairy world, where the ducks are eating all the blackberries, and they're getting drunk, and they're going around shouting like they've just won at football: 'We've got Green Heads!/ We've got Yellow Beaks!/WE ARE DUCKS!/ And we don't give a f-/eather if you hate us, cos we're making noise./WE ARE DUCKS! We're the green-headed boys!' When I read this with the girls, we make quite a performance of the ducks, and basically think we're being more hilarious than that cat in *You've Been Framed* that fell backwards into the swimming pool. Trouble is, though, I basically know the story's too complicated. But I also think it'll be cowardly not to try it out. I grab the book and run.

The teacher assistant says: 'Right, everyone, this is Grace's daddy; he's going to read. You can start. *Billy*, sit up, and don't pick your nose.' I'm thinking: If I'm trying to hold their attention, I better do crowd control. Some Year Six people come in. 'Who's this one?' I say. 'He's too big to be here.' The kids laugh a bit. I think: Fine. I'll clown with them, and we'll have some fun. Grace says: 'Daddy, START.'

I start the book. The kids want to see the pictures, which are small, and bad. I did them myself, with felt tips. I want to abandon the book, and just perform the story. I get to my feet. The teachers eye me like I'm a rampaging rhinoceros. I try to act soft and unthreatening. I become very camp. The Year Six guys are whispering. I can just *tell* they're saying: 'This dad is *really gay*!' Grace says: 'Daddy. Sit down.' I sit down.

I'm feeling very nervous. I start reading the bit about the ducks. I sing. Everyone stares. Grace is making the most desperate sound I've ever heard in my life: she's laughing sycophantically. She's trying to show her class this is funny. She's fully aware that Daddy's dying a death. I can already imagine the teachers discussing it: 'Grace's daddy came in, and he was so self-centred he brought one of his *own* stories, which was just crude.' I'm failing as a storyteller, as a comedian and as a dad. Those are my three core skills. This is bad.

But suddenly it's over. The teacher says: 'Well done,' in the sort of guarded voice you'd use for a child who's just drawn a nude picture of their mum. I can barely look at my daughter I'm so ashamed. But she grabs my hand, and she starts skipping home. She's happy. She doesn't care that I screwed up. She's just proud that I came.

Rule 60: Accept death

March 2007, Andover and Muswell Hill

Thursday, 5 p.m. I'm packing. I have to fly out tomorrow evening to meet the writers, producers and costume department of *Sadie the Wolverine*. They need to make my Wolverine Suit. Apparently, I'm going to have streaks of grey in the hair on my wolverine head, a bit like a badger. I'm getting my head round three key facts about *Sadie the Wolverine*.

1. I'll have to move to Vancouver, and Liv doesn't want to go. The girls are just starting school. And she doesn't want to leave her job, since for so long she's had the only regular wage in the house. But, if I go alone, I could have an affair. The contract is for two years. That's a long time for a family to be apart.
2. Livy is going to have a baby while I'm away. We'll have money for the first time, so we'll be able to afford an au pair. It's the modern system: you can pay someone to look after your children, to clean your house, to walk your dog, to massage your wife. But it's more fun to do it all yourself.
3. *Sadie the Wolverine* makes *Balls of Steel* look like high-class entertainment. I'd rather stay in England and write, even if I earn nothing.

But I know I must go. For the last eight years, I've been watching my performing career die like a puppy drowning in a bucket, and this is a Big Break. I complete the packing, and drive to Andover for my last stand-up gig.

It's a perfect gig for reminding me of all I won't be missing. There's a pillar in front of the stage. The bar staff are talking. I'm supposed to be headlining, but I accidentally do a set that's only twelve minutes long. I apologize to the management. I refuse my fee. At midnight, I'm driving around Andover's forty-nine roundabouts boiling with self-hatred. I'm thinking: As a performer, I'm *dead*.

Next morning, 10 a.m. Friday. I wake with a feeling of shame more acute than any hangover. I can't get the failed gig out of my head. Everyone's going off to the woods to play, but I'm preoccupied. Even at the best of times, it takes me a while to drop what I was doing to start playing, and you can't always say: 'Sorry. Daddy's tired.' But this morning feels especially doom-laden, since it's my last day before Canada. I say to Liv: 'You go ahead. I've got to call the airport,' then I go to the garage to smoke a pipe. It melts away the shame. It sands down the edges of the world. It makes me ready to play.

I catch up with them as they're walking into the woods. Grace runs towards me. '*Daddy!*' she shouts. '*Let's start!*'

'Right!' I say, putting on my Play Voice, which is louder than normal. 'What are we playing?'

'Pirates!'

'Brilliant. Who are you?'

Her answer is a classic. '*I'm Mr Firebeard!*' she announces. I'm so pleased I kiss her. Firebeard is wearing wellies, red duffle coat and a sparkly hair clip.

'Who are you, Cass?'

'**I'm a sailor**,' says Cass, '**but I don't have a name.**'

'You're *The Sailor With No Name*.'

She's pleased. My kids aren't actors. They don't put on

voices. But their favourite moment, in all games, is the moment of casting. The bit where you imagine being someone else. That's the best bit. The rest is just padding.

'Who am I?' I say.

'You are a wicked pirate who we hate,' says Grace.

'**You're the prince,**' says Cass. '**You are called Deedee Locomachio.**'

I've read *Impro* by Keith Johnstone, so I know the secrets of play:

1. Mirror the person you're playing with.
2. If you get two ideas, connect them both.
3. Say 'yes' to all suggestions. They are all brilliant.
4. Don't try to come up with a great idea. Assume your partner has had a great idea already. Find out what it is.

'I'm Deedee Locomachio the wicked pirate,' I say, 'who's really a prince.' I love my role. I feel like Errol Flynn. 'Who is Mum?' I shout.

'**She's a princess who you love,**' says Sailor. She is as well. I love that woman.

'Perfect! Let's Beeeeeeeegin!'

Princess finds sticks we can use as guns. We run. We shoot. We shout pirate insults: 'I hate you, Firebeard. I wipe bogeys on your fiery beard!' Firebeard wants to avenge my insults by tying me to a tree. I run off. Then I hide behind a suitable tree, holding out the dog lead. Firebeard, cackling horribly, wraps me in the dog lead, and announces I must be burned to death. I help with the knots.

'**Hold on,**' shouts Sailor, running over, '**I will rescue you!**' But Sailor gets her wellies caught in her dress. Sailor falls. Sailor gets muddy knees. Sailor considers crying. But Sailor gets up, Sailor gloriously rescues me and we run off swearing eternal friendship. Then I'm shot by Firebeard. Bang.

'Sailor!' I gasp. 'Fetch Princess. I must kiss her before I die.'

Princess arrives. She kisses. She whispers: 'Café in ten minutes.' I die. I'm thinking: Why do I always have to die in these games?

'**I am Baby Wolf!**' shouts Cass. '**You are Daddy Wolf!**' I'm thinking: Oh, Lord! A new game's already started! Couldn't Locomachio be mourned? Cass is thinking: Locomachio is dead! Big deal! Maybe he needed to die, so he could turn into a wolf.

Just then I get a text from Jeff who arranged Andover. It says: 'Want gig in Bognor tonight?' I text back: 'Bugger Bognor.' It's an odd feeling to turn down work. I never do it normally. Then a thought strikes me. Maybe I could turn down going to Vancouver. Maybe I don't need to go to Canada in order to be a wolf. I catch up Liv.

She's holding Cass's hand, and she's looking relaxed and cool.

'Liv,' I say, 'do you want me to go to Canada?'

'No. But I don't want to hold back your career.'

'Don't we need the money?'

'I'd rather we were happy than rich. The money doesn't really matter. We'll find some, somewhere. I've always thought you'd be a rather marvellous male prostitute.'

'Well, thanks ... But I'm not sure I believe you. For our whole relationship, money has been our biggest problem. I can't turn down a chance to earn some.'

She looks at me for a long time. 'OK,' she says.

Grace: "this is a love heart with rain in it".

Me: "why is there rain in a love heart?"

Grace: "because there was a crack in it, and because it was raining."

Rule 61: Don't have sex with strangers (people who are promiscuous in their thirties were mostly ugly in their teens)

March 2007, Gatwick airport

Saturday morning. I'm at Gatwick airport, on my way to Canada. I watch a dad come out of Arrivals. Girl runs over. Dad kisses girl. Boy runs over. Dad beams, and picks up boy. Mum arrives. Dad kisses her briefly. They walk off. I'm thinking: NOOO, you fool! Kiss her first. Obviously, she's not as cute as them: that's WHY you must kiss her first.

As I walk through Check-in, I feel depressed. I think: We may be the best generation of parents ever. We've got Lauren Child, we've got Supernanny, but we're all going to divorce, cos dads won't kiss their wives first. For the last month, Liv's not been kissing me because I've grown a red-dish moustache, which, I think, makes me look like Earl from *My Name is Earl*. She says I look like a ginger poof. Then I feel even more depressed since I'm not going to see the family for a week. Then I'll be back for a fortnight. Then I'll be off for two years. That doesn't make me a great dad.

I check in, and then go through to Departures. My phone beeps. I've got a text from an actress called Elizabeth Hamilton. She's got a starring role in *Sadie the Wolverine*, and is on the same flight. She's playing a kind PE teacher who teaches Sadie martial arts. 'Meet me in the oyster bar,' she writes. 'I'm the one with the red hair.' Suddenly I can't help but feel curious. Red-headed women excite me. And travel is all about the search for fresh adventure. It always makes me horny.

I reach the oyster bar. There's no one with red hair. There's just a businessman who's assuring his telephone that he's going to be 'hitting the ground running'. I sit down and order a coffee. I look at the monitor giving aeroplane information. I see there's a problem with our flight.

I also see it's 10 a.m; 10 a.m., Saturday: that's normally my favourite time of the week. At 9.45, every Saturday, I drop Cass off at ballet school, and then Grace and I walk down the old train line, to the Magic Tree. The Magic Tree has a swing, and low-lying branches, and the power of granting all wishes. As we go there, we talk about whatever's bothering us. Last week, Grace told me she gets annoyed at lunchtime, because Oldina the Dinner Lady always makes her hurry her lunch, and she doesn't get time to finish her sandwiches. So we climbed into the branches, and we asked the Magic Tree to give Grace more peace, especially when she's eating lunch. I wish I was there now. The Magic Tree always gives me pleasure, but not as much as Grace does.

'Andrew Clover, the lucky four leaf!' says a well-spoken voice.

I look up. It's Elizabeth Hamilton. She is extremely beautiful. She looks about twenty-six. She has long red hair. She has large sensitive eyes, the eyes of a suffering saint. She has exquisite, plump breasts, which are modestly hidden under a thin jumper. She reaches forward and kisses me. She smells of expensive perfume. Her hair touches my cheek. It seems a little forward to kiss when you don't know some-one, but I remember I'm an actor now, and I'm going to be with this woman for a while.

'Did you hear?' says Elizabeth. 'There's a security risk. Our plane might not take off till this evening.'

'Oh. OK. What shall we do to pass the time?'

'Let's order champagne. I think we can afford it.'

So Elizabeth and I drink champagne together. Quickly, we're feeling a little drunk, and she's telling me everything. It's quite heady. There's no one so intoxicating as a new friend, and we're bonded by the adventure ahead of us. She's already been out to Canada. She's had the part for nearly two months. I realize that I've been cast at the last minute. Someone else must have dropped out. She tells me about the girl playing Sadie. She's a complete nightmare. She's fourteen, and has already starred in twenty films. She's followed everywhere by her mother, who's obsessed by money, famous people and macrobiotic diets.

Elizabeth tells me she has a young son, Zach, who's almost twelve months old. He is at home with her mum. She promises to show me a picture. That worries me. Being shown baby pictures is like receiving a present: you have to act delighted, and I always worry I won't be able to do it. But Zach is a beautiful child, and I say as much.

'Who is his dad?' I ask.

'Oh . . . he's the director of a film I did in Hungary.'

She tells me the name. He's called Paul. I auditioned for him once. He's in his early forties.

'Are you still together?'

'God, no.'

'Did he not want to stay with you?'

'Oh my God,' says Elizabeth. 'He did. We married. We were together for a year, but I couldn't really handle it.'

'Why?'

'It's a nightmare raising a child on your own, but . . . I couldn't have stayed with him. I was just . . . losing my fire.'

'I know what you mean. I think I've lost mine. But maybe I've still got a pilot light on.' I give Elizabeth a meaningful look when I say that. She laughs. I want her to laugh again. 'My libido has been locked away, like the Christmas decorations. In fact, my libido is like Christmas. My wife's happy to see it, since it's only once a year.'

She laughs again. She has white teeth, and a very pink tongue.

'Do you still see Paul?'

'Oh yes. Luckily, we're now really good friends.'

'Do you never want to go back to him?'

'No. You know what they say ... All comedies end in a marriage. So if you are married, you're in a tragedy, which ends in death.'

I fancy her even more now she's coining Wildean epigrams. Up to now, I've just felt lust towards this woman. Now I think it's love. Now God is pushing us together, urging me towards a life of wit, art and constant sex.

'My wife and I have been together for eight years,' I say. 'After a while, you don't have the desire to make love. You have more of a desire to fall asleep. My fantasy woman has huge breasts, which dispense hot chocolate. In the crevice of her breasts, she has a custard cream. Tattooed across her stomach, she has the last chapter of *Winnie-the-Pooh*.'

This is a line from my stand-up act, so I feel a little guilty saying it. Amongst comics, it's very bad form to repeat your material in normal company. It's a sign of insecurity. Liv would have spotted it, but Elizabeth doesn't know.

'Thank you for being so understanding,' she says, squeezing my hand, and not letting go. 'I'm so glad you're coming to Canada. Sometimes I get so lonely out there.'

I stare at my champagne. I realize that Elizabeth has just indicated that she'll sleep with me. She's also suggested that, if I didn't stay with her afterwards, she'd understand. I feel a sensation I've not had for a while, that little buzzy squirty feeling in my perineum. I'm getting turned on.

'You look worried,' says Elizabeth. She looks at me caringly. 'Are you scared about the security risk?'

No. I'm scared I'll get lonely in Canada. I'm scared you'll take me to your bed, and I'll place my cheek on your soft white stomach. I'm scared I'll ruin the life of my family. I don't say that. I rummage in my bag for my cigarettes. I notice the gifts that the girls have given me. Livy has made me an egg and lettuce sandwich, which is my favourite. Cassady has given me a packet of coloured pencils, so I can draw her a picture of the plane. Grace has given me Bear Bear. I told her I couldn't take Bear Bear, but she said that Bear Bear likes snow, and he wanted to come with me.

I look up. To my surprise, Elizabeth is crying.

'What's the matter?' I say.

'I hope Zach is going to be OK. He's with my mum. But I don't like leaving him.'

'I'm sure he'll be fine.' I hug her.

'Thank you,' she says. With my arms still round her, I look into her suffering saint eyes. They are hazel, and they have little flecks of green. I can smell the champagne on her breath. Her lips open.

We kiss. It's officially on the cheek, but the edges of our mouths touch slightly. Her lips are moist, and very soft. I hold it a moment and smell her perfume. I want to kiss her ear, which has a freckle on it.

'I'm going to go and look for some CDs,' I say. I get up, and walk over to HMV, and I call up my agent's mobile. He doesn't answer.

I leave a message: 'Richard, it's Andrew Clover here. Listen. I'm very sorry about this, but I don't want to go to

Canada. I'm wondering if it's too late to pull out. Would you call me back as soon as you can?'

Then I call Liv. She's out as well. I remember that she's going to a school fête. She's running a catch-the-duck stall with James, the perfect dad, the one who understands allotments and earns loads of cash as a top corporate lawyer. Maybe she's flirting with him. Maybe their arms are brushing as they handle the plastic water fowl. I leave a similar message. I also tell her I'm going to have to stay at the airport till I can sort out my luggage. Then I look over at Elizabeth, who's touching up her eye make-up. I only left home this morning and already I've nearly got off with someone. I go and do what every guilty man does at an airport: I buy presents.

For Cass, I buy a DVD of *The Little Mermaid*. For Grace I get an audio CD of *The Secret Seven*. Then I remember that the CD drive doesn't work in our music machine. I go to Dixon's and buy a new one. Then for Liv, I buy a beige detective mac, which has a belt. Now I've got so many presents, I buy a cheap sack to put everything in.

Then I go to the British Airways desk to tell them I'm not going on the flight. They take my request well. Because of the security threat, several people have pulled out already. They tell me the luggage will be unloaded onto Carousel Eight.

I return to Elizabeth.

'Elizabeth,' I say. 'I've decided I'm not going to Canada.'

'What, *never*?'

'Never. I'm not going to be a Wolverine.'

'Oh my God,' she says, 'was it something I said?'

Of course it was.

'Of course not. I just don't think I'm an actor. I was only going out for the money. And maybe, if I don't go out, I'll find cash in some other way. But, listen, I really enjoyed meeting you. I hope you have a lovely time out there.'

'Thanks.'

We kiss again. It's on the lips this time. I figure I'm not going to see her again, so there's less danger. Then I walk to the carousel, and wait for my luggage. The drink is wearing off now, and I'm feeling tired. I take off my coat, and I lie on the plastic seats, and decide to sleep.

I close my eyes, and I immediately have a luscious dream about Elizabeth Hamilton. We're in a hotel room in Canada. I undo her jeans, and discover some red pants that Livy used to wear when we first met. As soon as I see those pants, I wake up, feeling startled and hung over, and ashamed.

I see where I've gone wrong. I've been saying kids teach you happiness because they make you see everything as if for the first time, and I've not been doing that with my own wife. I've been like a billionaire bored with his helicopter. I've been taking her for granted. I've been utterly forgetting how I used to feel about her, before I had kids, or a stupid moustache. I even wonder if I've been refusing to be sexy with her as part of some weird power struggle. I realize I'm lazy. Suddenly I picture my wife. I know now it's my marital duty to treat her like a red-headed prostitute. Once in a while. Now I feel like a sexy Viking returning from his travels.

I get a text. It says: 'Stay there. We're coming to pick you up! L X'. I've got one other thing to do before I leave the airport. I go to Boots and buy myself shaving things. I go to the toilet, and look at my reflection in the mirror. I have tufts of white hair growing on my ears. How is it that Livy has stayed loyal to a man like this? I shave off my ginger moustache.

When I get back, the luggage is waiting for me. I pick it

up, and walk through security. The lady customs officer wants to look through it. 'You're going to have to empty your sack,' she says.

'*Tell* me about it!' I say. She gives me a bad look.

Then I stride into Arrivals, and I see the whole family.

For a joke, they're all wearing wigs. Cassady's got a Kevin Keegan mullet, but I ignore her. Grace is wearing one of those tartan hats that have ginger hair sticking out the side. I ignore her too. Liv's wearing a blonde bob, which is hilarious, and very sexy. I kiss her softly on the lips, and, in that moment, she's a fresh bride in red pants, and life is a comedy, which can be enjoyed again and again and again.

In that moment life is a comedy which can be enjoyed again and again and again.

Rule 62: Remember the worm book

April 2007, Muswell Hill

Tuesday night. Ten p.m. I'm still writing. *Dirty Angels* has been sent to the publishers, but I want to do a couple of last tweaks. Liv appears. 'Right,' she says. 'I have to do loads of work first thing in the morning. You have to be up by seven. Now. Listen. You know Grace is supposed to give back the worm book.'

'What?!'

'You know ... the *worm book* ... The WORM BOOK!' She's shouting at me now, like that's gonna make it any easier to understand. 'The LIBRARY BOOK!'

'Oh, the library book. Yes. Fine.' I write it down. 'Return library book.' She says a few more things, but I'm not really listening. I'm just nodding and pretending to listen. Suddenly she's gone silent. 'Anything else?' I say.

'Yes! Can you come to bed?' she says, but not enticingly. She says it in the voice you'd use on a child who's just set fire to your tea towel.

Wednesday morning. We're all still in bed at 7.40. Suddenly, both girls appear. The atmosphere is, immediately, *very full on*.

Cass is shouting: '**But, Mummy, I am cold!**' And Grace is shouting: 'But I'm still tired!' And Liv is saying: 'Go to bed and doze!' and Grace is shouting: 'DOZE? Doze? What does doze mean?' and I'm leaping across the room eagerly seeking that library book like a dog chasing a rabbit. I get downstairs. I put on porridge, coffee and Johnny Cash's 'I Walk the Line', which has an irresistibly jaunty rhythm. Grace appears first. Grinning. She's decided she doesn't need to doze, but is ready to dance. We start a bobbing-on-the-spot dance. Then Liv arrives. She's carrying Cass under her arm, the way some people carry terriers. Cass is holding a box filled with bears. '**But this music is waking my BEARS!**' she shouts, immediately furious. Liv turns the music off. We all defer to the wishes of Cassady's bears.

Then it really kicks off. Spoons are chucked, sugar is sprayed, threats are made. At one point Cassady hurls her bowl to the floor, and lies there, stiff as a board. I rush upstairs, and search desperately for the library book. Liv arrives. She yanks out a drawer, which hits me on the head. 'For *God's* sake,' she says, 'you're supposed to be dressing them!'

Eventually we get outside where the fresh air hits us all like Valium and, immediately, we relax. Grace says, 'Ah, now THAT is a MYSTERY,' and points out a hairband fallen on the pavement. This is because I made up a story, last week, about Grace The Famous Detective. She's trying to give me more material.

And then we walk down this alleyway, which leads to the school. It's got three bollards at the top to stop people driving down it. Cass has got names for all three of them. She pats them: '**Hello, Doodoo. Hello, Deedee. Hello, Pom.**' I see our local celebrity, Steve Pemberton from *The League of Gentlemen*. He smiles. We skip.

When we get to the playground, I realize I've forgotten the library book, but I don't care. Everyone's wearing bright coats and they're smiling and saying hello. I feel extremely happy. It's partly because it's a beautiful morning with crisp winter light. And it's also because being a parent is like being a breakfast DJ: the hard part of the day comes first. But by nine o'clock the difficult work is done, and you can enjoy yourself.

When I get home, I see Liv through the kitchen window. She's slicing banana into my porridge. I love banana in porridge. I love Liv. I have a thought I've never had before. I think: If I were in heaven, how would it be different? I can't think of anything.

My phone rings. My agent has sold *Dirty Angels* to a publisher. The money isn't great, but it'll keep us in princess shoes for a month or so. I go in and tell Liv. She's delighted. She thinks we should go away for a celebratory holiday. We decide we'll go to Bilbao, but then we calculate we don't have enough cash. So then we decide we'll go to Margate. Then we decide we'll holiday in London. We'll stay at her mum's house. We'll get her mum to play along. She'll have to put little shampoo bottles next to our bed. When we arrive at her house, she has to say: 'You're treating this place like a hotel!'

That night, I tell the girls the good news. Grace is very proud. Cassady is furious we haven't sold the book that is about her. I celebrate by getting in the bath with them. They show me how to use the slippy end as a slide. Afterwards, they want stories. I'm feeling so confident, I make one up off the top of my head. It's about this poor woodcutter who finds some treasure just when he realizes he doesn't need it. He's got everything he needs, right here, right now.

Rule 63: Do Nothing

May 2007, Muswell Hill

Grace recently started a new book, which is called *A Mystery Book. The Missing Jewels*, By Grace Clover (Detective). She did the cover page a week ago. Every day since, she's got her book out, and all she's done is number the pages. She's currently reached 44.

This afternoon I'm watching her numbering.

I say to her: 'What's *The Missing Jewels* going to be about?'

She says: 'I'm not doing the story yet. I'm doing the numbers.'

'But don't you need to know the story?'

'You can't do the story,' she explains, 'till you've done the numbers.'

'Do you think writers always do the numbers first?'

'Yes. Otherwise they can't start.'

Suddenly I'm getting worried that The Drop has happened: she's getting self-conscious; she's lost her childish inventiveness. Creativity is like stretching, or like having fun: it's something that all kids can do, but then most of them lose the ability. It's distressing.

'But, Grace,' I say, '*who* is in the story?'

'Ah!' she says. 'It's about a jewel thief called Joel Garner. And he's got red clothes, and black boots, and a bag that smells of wee. He steals the jewels, and then he puts them in his bag, and then he gives them to princesses. But they're embarrassed because of the wee, and they don't really want them.'

'Grace! That's a brilliant story,' I say. I can't say how relieved I feel. I honestly thought she'd started clamming up.

I say: 'Shall we start writing the story?'

'No,' she says. 'I'm having fun doing the numbers.'

In a flash I recognize a terrible truth. I've always believed that I don't push the children at all because I don't care if they're good at maths, or if they're rubbish at running. I went to Oxford University, and still ended up miserable and so broke that I had to search the gutters for spare change. All that matters, I reckon, is that they find out what they like doing, and have a positive attitude towards it. Now I see I've been pushing my daughters to be professional authors, and I've been setting them a very tight deadline. I must stop.

Cassady is busy playing with my dressing-gown cord. For the sixth week running, that's top of the charts: the most popular toy. She's tied it between a chair and her bike, and now she's sticking hair clips along it.

'Do you want to do some painting, Cassady?' I say.

'**No**,' she says. '**I need to do this. It's a tightrope for bears.**'

And so I stop fussing, and I watch them. They're like trees. They're pushing out their branches, and they're finding their own shape. I watch them some more, and then we go upstairs and bath, and then we do stories. Tonight we read the last chapter of *The House at Pooh Corner*. The one where Christopher Robin asks Pooh, 'What do you like doing best in the world?' and Pooh answers, 'What I like *doing* best is Me and Piglet going to see You, and You saying, "What about a little something?"' 'I like that too,' says Christopher Robin. 'But what I like *doing* best is nothing.'

Christopher Robin is leaving the Hundred Acre Wood to go to school. He's leaving childhood. It reminds you of *Peter Pan*, where J. M. Barrie says that, when you're two, you forget how to fly. 'Two is the beginning of the end.' That kills me. And, at first glance, the end of *The House at Pooh Corner* is similarly destructive. Except it isn't really, because Christopher Robin's grasped the most important thing that you must remember if you want to return to the enchanted place: you first have to do Nothing. And if adults learn how to do it, they'll find they can go there too.

Afterword

June 2007

I've just checked through this manuscript, before sending it to my publisher. I realized, belatedly, that this book is all about finding your inner child, and I suddenly wondered if I'd really captured it.

Just then, Cassady barged in.

'**Daddy,**' she said. '**You wish you were a child, don't you, Daddy? If you want to be a child, then you must DRESS UP, because if you dress up you have a more nice day. When we dress up we have a more nicer time, than grown-ups. You see, Daddy? Write that. Write it, Daddy.**'

I looked at her, astonished. I was thinking: How the *hell* does she know what I'm writing about?

'Is there anything else I should write?' I said.

'**Nuffink,**' she said. '**Write nuffink.**'

Postscript

August 2007

The delivery room is quiet. Livy is bouncing gently on a big rubber ball, sucking sensuously on the gas and air. She looks like she's on a space hopper, and she's smoking a bong. I feel jealous.

I ask the midwife: 'Are dads allowed gas and air?'

'Don't let me see you doing it,' she says. 'But I would say . . . you need four deep drags to really get the benefit.'

She leaves. I have eight deep ones. I *really* get the benefit. My head is light. My heart beats. I stare at my wife with her loose hair and her flushed cheeks and I don't think I've ever loved her so much.

'*The gas!*' she shouts. 'Stop hogging it!'

She inhales furiously. The midwife returns. 'I'm going to examine you,' she says. I think she's referring to me for a second.

She inserts her hand between Livy's legs. She goes white. She leaves, and returns with two doctors. One after the other they insert their hands into Livy. What is it about doctors? Whenever I meet one, they fist my wife. They don't even enjoy it. They look terrified.

'What?!' I say. 'What's wrong?'

'The baby's got a lump on her head,' says a doctor. They leave.

I feel weak. I notice three signs on the wall about shoulder dystocia. That's when the shoulders get stuck; the baby is throttled by the vagina. I try to calm myself by looking through the free present bag. It contains a brochure advertising ugly expensive plates that give the baby's name, weight and date of birth. I see another sign. It says: 'Please collect umbilical cords for use in clinical tests.' Our baby isn't born yet. Already she's being sold to. Already she's being used. Already she's sick.

My wife screams. I pass her the water. I pass her the gas. She grabs my hand and she mangles the knuckles together. Don't get me wrong. I know she's suffering more than me, but couldn't my job be done by a bedpost? My hand is going to need surgery.

'It's coming,' says the midwife. 'Liv, kneel up and face the wall. Andrew, you're helping delivery. Place your hands on mine.'

I go down the business end. The next contraction opens the womb. I see ooze and offal and terrifying matter. Liv speaks in the flat strangled tones of the dalek: *I can't do it!* Suddenly, a purple head appears. It pauses, as if contemplating Liv's buttock. I hold it with the midwife and we gently wiggle the shoulders past the throttling lips. Liv yells again, and the baby slides out like a wet mermaid coming down a pipe. She starts as she means to carry on: she shits and starts screaming.

She's out. She's got a small skin flap on her head. She's covered in slime. But she's alive. She's out, she's ours and she's alive.

The midwife wraps her swiftly. I take her to the edge of the room. I can't stop myself. I start whispering into her tiny bloody ear: 'Darling ... Darling ... I'm going to take you home and you're going to meet a person called Cassady. Yes I am. I'm going to take you to Hackney Downs to see the longest swings in London. Yes I am. And I'm going to take you on holiday, and you're going to get the first exhilarating sight of the sea. Yes you are. Oh, you strange bald-headed goblin, with your weird bubble of skin, we're going to have *so* much fun together.'

The Dad Rules

Find a woman. Follow her, to hospital if necessary. Give
her love. Generosity is its own reward, specially if you're
giving out loving, and she's wearing the bunny ears. Give
her an inch, she'll chuck you; give her six, she'll breed. Two
cells become four cells which become someone who will
wipe jam on your CDs. They have arrived like a messenger.
Listen to them, unless they start shouting. Say 'Yes' to
everything, even wigs. Join in. When in Rome, get
sunglasses, and a Fiat, and drive round looking for toilets.
When home, drop to the floor, and let them ride you
round the bedroom. Don't get scared. Get agoraphobic.
Shut the door. Disconnect the phone. Know that the
party is here. You may as well enjoy it, you'll be tidying up.
You can lead a horse to water, you can't make him pick up jelly.
Don't invite too many guests, specially if they come with mums.
Children are like farts, if they're yours they're surprisingly
lovely; they remind you of you; when other people's appear,
it's best to leave the room. Relax. Be patient.
Whenever, and wherever possible, do Nothing.

RACHEL JOHNSON

THE MUMMY DIARIES

Rachel Johnson lives in Notting Hill with her three children, husband and her dog, Coco. This, she sometimes needs to remind herself, is a good thing.

For if the endless succession of school runs, birthday parties (including one for Coco), meal times, shopping trips, skirmishes over undone homework, second-home trials and au pair tribulations doesn't get her, then deciding to keep a diary of her social, school and holiday year probably will. What follows is a hilarious and heartwarming rendition of a year with a not-so-ordinary Notting Hill family trying desperately to live an ordinary life.

'Wonderful! Such joy, such giggles…Johnson writes beautifully and I thank her for cheering me up' Jilly Cooper

'Deliciously complicit…a sprightly footnote to the official history of our strange times' *Sunday Telegraph*

'Johnson's self-deprecating style makes this an irresistible read' *Babyworld*

'Very, very funny…you get the distinct impression Johnson is making up this whole wife/mother thing as she goes along' *Heat*

read more

JUDITH O'REILLY

WIFE IN THE NORTH

350 miles from home, three young children and one very absent husband …

Maybe hormones ate her brain. How else did Judith's husband persuade her to give up her career and move from her beloved London to Northumberland with two toddlers in tow?

Pregnant with number three, Judith is about to discover that there are one or two things about life in the country that no one told her about: that she'd be making friends with people who believe in the four horsemen of the apocalypse; that running out of petrol could be a near-death experience; and that the closest thing to an ethnic minority would be a redhead.

Judith tries to do that simple thing that women do, make hers a happy family. A family that might live happily ever after. Possibly even up North …

'Funny, poignant and beautifully written' Lisa Jewell

'I howled with laughter, tears of recognition at every page' Jenny Colgan

'Genuinely funny and genuinely moving' Jane Fallon

CATHERINE SANDERSON

PETITE ANGLAISE

In Paris. In Love. In Trouble.

English Rose Catherine Sanderson loved France so much she moved to Paris, where she got a job. Found a Frenchman – Mr Frog. And they had a child – Tadpole. Then one day, in an idle moment, Catherine spiced things up by creating a blog – and Petite Anglaise was born. But Petite had a life of her own. Soon, she was snatching illicit moments in seedy hotels with sexy online lover James before Catherine ran home for a guilty snuggle with Tadpole. Was daring, witty Petite having too much fun? What about Catherine's crumbling relationship with Mr Frog? She might be bilingual, but how long can an English Rose keep up a double life?

Petite Anglaise is the true story of how a mum found love and romance in Paris by becoming the girl she'd always wanted to be.

'I loved it' India Knight

'Addictively readable. A Thoroughly modern tale of life and love' *Mail on Sunday*

'Light, frank and tremendous fun. Like all good writers, Catherine's work enables us to appreciate the diversity, possibilities, trials and beauty of life' *Guardian*

LUCY CAVENDISH

LOST AND FOUND

Samantha Smythe has a busy summer ahead of her with her three active young sons. Her au pair is more interested in the contents of the fridge than in the children, her husband is off drinking champagne for breakfast in London, and the famous footballer who has moved into the village seems to think Samantha is the answer to his problems.

Then, out of the blue, Samantha's childhood friend Naomi turns up on the doorstep with her daughter in tow. It's been years since Samantha and Naomi have seen each other and it's not long before they fall back into their old ways. Samantha would do anything for Naomi but when she's left to look after her little girl as well has her own chaotic family, she has to ask herself what she is prepared to do to save a friendship.

Everyone has a long lost friend but what happens when the past comes back and turns your life upside down? Can things ever go back to the way they were?

Praise for *Samantha Smythe's Modern Family Journal*:

'A lightly amusing chick lit number about the trials of mummyhood' *Tatler*

'Fast paced…with a plot abundant in twists and turns' *Daily Telegraph*

'Keeps you gripped and entertained through to the end' *Daily Express*

read more ⓟ

NIAMH GREENE

SECRET DIARY OF A DEMENTED HOUSEWIFE

When Susie's maiden aunt gives her a housekeeping journal, she expects Susie to use it for jotting down nutritious recipes and planning household budgets. But Susie has more important things on her mind ...

... Like how to keep sane while trying to control a four-year-old diva who thinks she's Judy Garland, as well as a thrill-seeking toddler with a death wish. Not to mention managing a demanding husband who expects a home-cooked meal at least once a fortnight and inconsiderate parents who seem to think luxury spa breaks are more important than spending time with their grandchildren. On top of that, there's the small matter of the Lone Father at the children's play group who is clearly smitten and Susie's passing interest in Posh'n'Becks, Wayne and Colleen, Brad'n'Jen'n'Angelina ...

Susie's journal chronicles a hectic year in the life of a stay at home mother, whose one ambition is to possess an outfit that is free of snot stains.

'Hilariously written...will keep you laughing all the way' *Woman*

'Brilliantly astute' *OK!*

'Fab' *Closer*

www.penguin.com

Love letters?

Find someone whose words
could inspire you at
www.penguindating.co.uk

Discover your own happy ending.

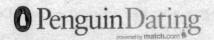

He just wanted a decent book to read ...

Not too much to ask, is it? It was in 1935 when Allen Lane, Managing Director of Bodley Head Publishers, stood on a platform at Exeter railway station looking for something good to read on his journey back to London. His choice was limited to popular magazines and poor-quality paperbacks – the same choice faced every day by the vast majority of readers, few of whom could afford hardbacks. Lane's disappointment and subsequent anger at the range of books generally available led him to found a company – and change the world.

'We believed in the existence in this country of a vast reading public for intelligent books at a low price, and staked everything on it'
Sir Allen Lane, 1902–1970, founder of Penguin Books

The quality paperback had arrived – and not just in bookshops. Lane was adamant that his Penguins should appear in chain stores and tobacconists, and should cost no more than a packet of cigarettes.

Reading habits (and cigarette prices) have changed since 1935, but Penguin still believes in publishing the best books for everybody to enjoy. We still believe that good design costs no more than bad design, and we still believe that quality books published passionately and responsibly make the world a better place.

So wherever you see the little bird – whether it's on a piece of prize-winning literary fiction or a celebrity autobiography, political tour de force or historical masterpiece, a serial-killer thriller, reference book, world classic or a piece of pure escapism – you can bet that it represents the very best that the genre has to offer.

Whatever you like to read – trust Penguin.

read more
www.penguin.co.uk